On Teaching Literature

ESSAYS FOR SECONDARY SCHOOL TEACHERS

Published for the
Indiana University English Curriculum Study Center
in cooperation with the
Indiana State Department of Public Instruction
RICHARD D. WELLS, *Superintendent*

On Teaching Literature

ESSAYS FOR SECONDARY SCHOOL TEACHERS

EDITED BY

EDWARD B. JENKINSON

Director, Indiana University
English Curriculum Study Center

AND

JANE STOUDER HAWLEY

Formerly Assistant Director,
Indiana University English
Curriculum Study Center

BLOOMINGTON *Indiana University Press* LONDON

72743

CONTENTS

ACKNOWLEDGMENTS

The portion of the project of the I.U. English Curriculum Study Center reported herein was supported through the Cooperative Research Program of the Office of Education, U. S. Department of Health, Education and Welfare.

Grateful acknowledgment is made to Professors Philip B. Daghlian and William H. Wiatt, both of the Department of English, Indiana University, for their help in planning this volume and for their assistance with the editing. Two secretaries—Mrs. Robert Spencer and Mrs. James Louden—quietly accepted the chore of retyping the many revisions of chapters and assisted with the proofreading.

Thanks also go to the Indiana State Department of Public Instruction for distributing this volume to teachers of English in Indiana.

Acknowledgment is also made to the publishers for permission to quote portions of the following poems and essays:

e. e. cummings, "Portrait VIII," from *Collected Poems,* © 1923. Reprinted by permission of Harcourt, Brace & World, Inc.

Irvin Ehrenpreis, "Why Literature Should Be Taught," from *Proceedings of the Philosophy of Education Society 1958,* © 1958. Reprinted by permission of the publisher of the *Proceedings,* Philosophy of Education Society, School of Education, University of Kansas.

T. S. Eliot, "The Waste Land," from *Collected Poems 1909–1962 by T. S. Eliot,* © 1963, 1st American Edition. Reprinted by permission of Harcourt, Brace & World, Inc.

Robert Frost, "To Earthward," from *Complete Poems of Robert Frost,* © 1923 by Holt, Rinehart and Winston, Inc., © 1951 by Robert Frost. Reprinted by permission of Holt, Rinehart and Winston, Inc.

Edgar A. Guest, "Failures," from *Collected Verse,* © 1934 by Reilly &

Lee Company, Chicago. Reprinted by permission of Henry Regnery Company, Publishers.

Gerard Manley Hopkins, "Spring and Fall," from *Reading Poems,* © 1941 by Oxford University Press. Reprinted by permission of Oxford University Press.

Robinson Jeffers, "Hurt Hawks," from *Modern American Poetry,* © 1919, 1921, 1925, 1930, 1936, 1942 by Harcourt, Brace & Company. Reprinted by permission of Random House, Inc., Alfred A. Knopf, Inc.

Philip Larkin, "Toads," from *New Poets of England and America,* © 1957. Reprinted by permission of Meridian Books.

Archibald MacLeish, "Ars Poetica," from *Poems, 1924–1933,* © 1925, 1926, 1928, 1932, and 1933 by Archibald MacLeish. Reprinted by permission of Houghton Mifflin Company.

Archibald MacLeish, *Land of the Free,* © 1938, 1966 by Archibald MacLeish. Reprinted by permission of Harcourt, Brace & World, Inc.

John Myers, Jr., "Intimations of Mortality: An Analysis of Hopkins' 'Spring and Fall'," from *Modern Poetry in the Classroom,* © 1961–1963. Reprinted by permission of the author and the National Council of Teachers of English.

Howard Nemerov, *Poets on Poetry,* © 1966. Reprinted by permission of the author.

Howard Nemerov, "The View from an Attic Window," from *New & Selected Poems,* © 1960 the University of Chicago Press. Reprinted by permission of the author.

Wilfred Owen, "Anthem for Doomed Youth," from *Collected Poems,* © 1963 by Chatto & Windus Ltd. Reprinted by permission of New Directions Publishing Corporation.

Wilfred Owen, "Dulce Et Decorum Est," from *Collected Poems,* © 1963 by Chatto & Windus Ltd. Reprinted by permission of New Directions Publishing Corporation.

Ezra Pound, "Canto I," from *The Cantos,* © 1934 by Ezra Pound. Reprinted by permission of New Directions Publishing Corporation.

John Crowe Ransom, "Here Lies a Lady," from *New Anthology of Modern Poetry,* © 1938 by Random House, Inc. Reprinted by permission of Random House, Inc., Alfred A. Knopf, Inc.

John Crowe Ransom, "The Equilibrists," from *Chief Modern Poets of England & America,* © 1943, 3rd edition, by the Macmillan Company. Reprinted by permission of Random House, Inc., Alfred A. Knopf, Inc.

Edwin Arlington Robinson, "Mr. Flood's Party," from *Chief Modern Poets of England & America,* © 1943, 3rd edition, by the Macmillan Company. Reprinted by permission of The Macmillan Company.

Dylan Thomas, "Altarwise by Owl-light," from *Collected Poems,* © 1953 by Dylan Thomas. Reprinted by permission of New Directions Publishing Corporation.

Dylan Thomas, "Poem in October," from *Collected Poems,* © 1939 by New Directions Publishing Corporation. Reprinted by permission of New Directions Publishing Corporation.

Dylan Thomas, "Do not go gentle into that good night," from *Collected Poems,* © 1953 by Dylan Thomas. Reprinted by permission of New Directions Publishing Corporation.

Richard Wilbur, "A Simile for Her Smile," from *Ceremony and Other Poems,* © 1948, 1949, 1950 by Richard Wilbur. Reprinted by permission of Harcourt, Brace & World, Inc.

William Carlos Williams, "The Red Wheelbarrow," from *Collected Earlier Poems,* © 1938 by William Carlos Williams. Reprinted by permission of New Directions Publishing Corporation.

James Wright, "Saint Judas," from *Saint Judas: poems,* © 1959, 1st edition. Reprinted by permission of Wesleyan University Press.

On Teaching Literature
ESSAYS FOR SECONDARY SCHOOL TEACHERS

1

An Introduction for School Administrators

EDWARD B. JENKINSON

Coordinator for School English Language Arts;
Director of the Indiana University
English Curriculum Study Center

Two years ago secondary school teachers of English, experimenting with materials prepared in the Indiana University English Curriculum Study Center, requested that an able teacher-scholar be asked to write an essay on teaching the novel that would serve as a useful guide for them. Professor George Levine of Indiana University's Department of English agreed to attempt an essay that "might be of some value." So enthusiastic was the response to the Levine essay that the director of the Indiana University Center asked five other successful teacher-scholars to write essays on teaching short stories, poetry, drama, essays, and biography.

All six essays in this volume attempt to give busy secondary school teachers effective approaches to the teaching of literature. The six essayists were not given specific guidelines. Instead, each was free to approach his topic as he saw fit. The results, of course, represent occasional disparities of opinion and differences in tone that are not only expected but welcomed in such a volume. But all six contributors underscore these obvious facts:

1. The able teacher of literature champions no single method of

teaching novels, short stories, poems, plays, essays, or biographies but, instead, carefully studies each work, both in terms of its genre and as an individual work of art, before deciding how to present it to his students.

2. The conscientious teacher of literature reads not just one essay on teaching the novel, for example, but books of essays that give him fresh insights into novels and how to approach them in his classroom.

3. The successful teacher of literature realizes that good teaching demands a great deal of time, hard work, and intelligence.

Each of the six essayists assumes that his audience consists of teachers who have the desire, and will eventually have the time, to do a superior job of teaching literature. For example, Professor Levine writes:

> All one can do in teaching a novel, it seems to me, is hope to put the students on the right track by asking the right questions, by establishing broad general outlines (by means of examples, of course) into which the rest of the novel can be fit with least distortion, and by making the right demands of the book. Far from presuming, then, to try to formulate some definitive mode of teaching the novel, or to define the novel, I should like rather to make a few suggestions about the kinds of discriminations one needs to make while teaching novels, the kinds of questions which might fairly be asked of all novels, and the possible ways of leading a student from consideration of the novel as a raw chunk of life to consideration of it as form and meaning.

In those two sentences Professor Levine asks a great deal of his reader. He assumes that a teacher will carefully reread any novel he is teaching and that he will be able to discuss each novel's form and its possible meanings. Implicit in those two sentences is the further assumption that the teacher will have studied criticism of the novel so that he can, in forming his questions and in explaining the novel's form and possible meanings, take to his classroom the best thinking of the most able scholars.

The careful formation of challenging questions is not limited to the teaching of fiction. Professor Donald Peet notes:

> The teacher who requires his students to present oral or written book reports will have frequent opportunities to illuminate the problem of biography in general by the suggestions he makes when students are preparing reports on biographical narratives and by the questions he asks when these reports are delivered or handed in. By asking his students how the biographer whose book they have been reading came to possess the knowledge he displays, and by inquiring as to the evidence this biographer cites to substantiate his conclusions, the teacher may stimulate students to ask the same kind of questions themselves in their future reading. By so doing, the teacher will have taken an important step toward producing readers who actively analyze the implications of what they read instead of passively absorbing whatever they find on the page before them.

No teacher could aspire to do more than to lead students to "actively analyze the implications of what they read." But students cannot be led to such analysis by questions like these, paraphrased from a teacher's guide to *A Tale of Two Cities*:

1. Why was Charles Darnay on trial? A. treason; B. larceny; C. arson; D. murder.
2. Who tells the story of the murderer's death? A. Defarge; B. the woodsawyer; C. an unknown observer; D. the mender of roads.

Such questions can only convince students that a superficial reading of any work is sufficient. But questions like these, taken from a student edition of *A Tale of Two Cities*, help students to plumb the depths of meaning, to appreciate, and to better understand a work of art:

1. In times of war and social upheaval individual persons often seem to be swept along on a tide of forces beyond their control. How does the phrasing of the last sentence in this chapter manage to suggest the helplessness of the persons in this story to govern their own destinies?

2. *A wonderful fact to reflect upon, that every human creature is constituted to be that profound secret and mystery to every other.* Show that this sentence, which opens Chapter 3, expresses the theme of the entire chapter.

Forming such questions, which takes time and a sensitivity to literature, is of extreme importance in teaching literature, as Professor Mary Alice Burgan notes: "The art of teaching seems to me a matter of questions and answers; the best teachers I have known have been the ones who could outguess me—tell me what questions I was asking. I have tried to do some wholesale 'outguessing' here because I have found that my own teaching has been most successful when I have had a relatively 'antagonistic' group of students to work with—and by 'antagonistic' I mean students who were either 'stumped' or convinced that they could not 'get' English literature."

Without the right questions, without questions that stimulate thinking, students become antagonistic in a manner that would appall Professor Burgan. Outright antagonism toward, and boredom with, English result from a steady diet of questions like this:

As he fights Valvert, what does Cyrano do? A. composes a poem; B. makes complimentary remarks about Valvert's swordsmanship; C. compliments the ladies in the audience; D. eats some pastries.

Fed such pablum, a student is not prepared to read a work closely and to analyze it thoroughly. He is far from being prepared to answer questions like these that Professor Gerald Rabkin would ask of any work of art: "What is the author getting at? What means does he use to communicate his concerns? How effectively does he communicate them? How significant are the concerns themselves? How imaginatively has he used the conventions of the particular genre in which he has chosen to work?" Such questions tax both teacher and student; they require the teacher to be so well read that he can lead the students to acceptable answers.

But why this preoccupation with questions? Is it not true that too much analysis of a literary work causes students to dislike literature? Professor Don Cook says no.

[Rigorous] analysis does not, I think, destroy aesthetic pleasure. If we help the student to conceive of the essay in the terms Montaigne proposed, that is as a trial flight of an idea and of a mind, then much of the pleasure will derive from seeing the idea stay aloft. What keeps it aloft? What prevents its descending into banality, dullness, or obscurity? What powers its flight and gives it buoyancy? These are the questions that arouse and engage the critical perception. And finally, as he comes to recognize the techniques and devices of the writer and to experience the vicarious pleasures of watching ideas hatched, fledged, and launched, a student may be moved to try his own powers of creation.

Whether he writes only class-assigned themes or tries to write short stories, essays, and poems, the student-writer must be a sensitive reader if he is to improve his own work as well as to react critically to the work of others. The student who resists such analysis will probably never be an intelligent reader or writer of prose and poetry, as Professor Philip Appleman indicates:

No matter how simple and nontechnical we make our discussion, though, some students will call it "picking the poems apart" (not a bad definition, by the way, of the word "analysis"). They mean, of course, that they don't like it and think it shouldn't be done at all: they would apparently prefer simply to gasp in ecstacy at poems they immediately like and shrug off those they dislike. This sort of reacting may have some virtues, but they are not the virtues that will, in the long run, help the estate of poetry. The simple reactor-to-poetry is necessarily either a critical anarchist, for whom discussion and communication are irrelevant or impossible, or a kind of incipient dictator, who believes that everyone else ought to respond in the same way he does. In either case, his attitude precludes the possibility of talking about the good and bad qualities of particular poems.

To change such a student's attitude, the teacher of literature must be skilled in the art of forming questions, in the art of analysis, and in the art of teaching. And he must have the time to read

and reread to understand the work thoroughly and to prepare
questions for his students.

Much has been written about the reduction of class loads for
teachers of English. The National Council of Teachers of English,
the Modern Language Association, the Commission on English of
the College Entrance Examination Board, and other national and
state organizations have suggested that no teacher of English be
assigned more than four classes with a total of 100 students. Most
of the arguments for class-load reduction are based on the paper-
grading load of the teacher, which is formidable.

Like the close reading of literature, the evaluation of themes is
time-consuming. Carefully read and evaluated, a theme of 250
words takes at least ten minutes of a teacher's time. Give him 150
themes to read outside class each week and the teacher spends at
least 25 hours at that task alone. He has precious little time left
for reading literature as carefully as the essayists in this volume
suggest that he must if he is to perform successfully in the classroom.

The essayists in this volume are concerned with the superior
teaching of literature. Future volumes in this series will be concerned with the superior teaching of composition, syntax, usage,
semantics, dialects, phonemes, morphemes, logic, and lexicography
as well as literature. To teach these subjects well requires a great
deal of time, and it therefore seems appropriate to make a plea
now for the reduction of class loads. The reading, paper-grading,
and preparation loads of a good teacher of English are so great
that he cannot possibly perform well in a classroom if he has a
crippling load of five classes with 125 students a day, or, worse, an
inhuman load of five, six, or seven classes with 150 to 225 students
a day. New curriculum materials, new textbooks, new books of
criticism, new audio-visual aids, and new books like this one, will
be of little value to the teacher if he does not have time to read,
to think, and to prepare. Quality education depends upon good
teachers who have the time to strive for excellence.

2

On Teaching the Novel

GEORGE LEVINE

Associate Professor of English,
Indiana University

The novel, which grew up traditionless and almost at popular request, is the only one of the major literary forms that retains any significant portion of its earlier popularity. It is still possible— though rare—to write a genuinely important novel and expect to sell a good many copies. Of course, one hundred years ago the novel had a position in relation to popular entertainment similar to that of television today, and it will never regain that sort of popularity. But because the novel persistently refuses to settle down into a single traditional form, and because its very tradition of popularity impels even the most avant-garde novelist to include elements of rather conventional human interest—adventure, comedy, the development of a human personality, and so on—the novel is perhaps the best possible form by which to lead reluctant and television-trained young men and women into literature.

Of all the literary forms, the novel makes its appeal most directly and unashamedly to life itself, and I confess personally to being a little tired of hearing how the life of any work of art is so exclusively in the language on the page that it cannot be carried over into the common experience of everyday living. Indeed, one of the central problems of fiction is to work out how novels so often manage to convey the impression of life itself and how much of that ordinary experience one needs to bring to novels in order to make them comprehensible. I shall, as anyone who has heard academic discussions of literature before knows, have to qualify these ideas and argue for the importance of the study of form, but I do feel strongly that in the teaching of the novel it is almost never a mistake to use the ordinary interests of students and to allow them, if cautiously, to make cross-references to their own experience as they so incorrigibly and humanly insist on doing.

But the peculiarly popular quality of fiction—especially of the fiction that gets taught in high schools—has its dangers. The novel's resistance to hardening of form makes it a genre especially difficult to define and to criticize according to any generally applicable principles. Indeed, to call the novel a form at all is misleading, since there are so many different kinds of books which get themselves called novels that the word "novel" is frequently without any meaning at all. It used to be that one could say that the novel was (a) a long story, and (b) in prose. Now the notion of telling a story has lost its artistic respectability, and the language of poetry and the language of prose have become in many cases indistinguishable.

The novel is thus also a peculiarly difficult form to teach. The methods one uses—insofar as one can be said to have a method—to teach *Madame Bovary* cannot and ought not be the same as those one uses to teach, say Joyce's *Portrait of the Artist*. Both of these books need to be taught differently from *The Scarlet Letter*, and that from *Moby Dick*, and that from *Huckleberry Finn*, and so on.

On top of these difficulties, there is the difficulty of the sheer length of most novels. Obviously, while it is possible to hold a lyric poem before the student since it is all on one page or perhaps two or three, one cannot hold a 500-page novel before him. And no art form depends so heavily on the accumulation of great basketloads of details, any one of which may seem at first sight to have relevance to nothing but itself, as the novel. It would seem to follow then that there is no hope of teaching a novel, and that the teacher must reconcile himself to doing at the very best a job so incomplete that ninety per cent of even the most important things in the book cannot be discussed. I think it really does follow. All one can do in teaching a novel, it seems to me, is hope to put the students on the right track by asking the right questions, by establishing broad general outlines (by means of examples, of course) into which the rest of the novel can be fit with least distortion, and by making the right demands of the book. Far from presuming, then, to try to formulate some definitive mode of teaching the novel, or to define the novel, I should like rather to make a few suggestions about the kinds of discriminations one needs to make while teaching novels, the kinds of questions which might fairly be asked about almost all novels, and the possible ways of leading a student from consideration of the novel as a raw chunk of life to consideration of it as form and meaning.

The tendency of most students when they read a novel is to become absorbed in the characters and to think of them as real people. This is, as I have already suggested, altogether comprehensible and not necessarily unfortunate. The tradition of the novel from *Robinson Crusoe* to the present has been for the most part to insist on the reality of the experience it describes. Novels aren't usually about kings and queens or heroic knights, but about people engaged in the kinds of activities an ordinary middle-class man might recognize. Unfortunately, since this is the case, a student will tend to dismiss a book if the characters don't behave as he expects ordinary people to behave, or he will find a novel good because they do.

Again, there is no point in not taking advantage of this kind of interest, but it needs to be handled carefully. The kind of discussion appropriate to Elizabeth Bennett in *Pride and Prejudice*, or, to a lesser extent, to Pip in *Great Expectations*, is off the point for Catherine Earnshaw in *Wuthering Heights*. The first two characters are deliberately placed in settings which are recognizable to an ordinary man and which place them socially. They are in part defined by their social positions. Their thoughts and actions seem consistently within the bounds (or comprehensible in terms) of normal experience, and the experience through which they go develops and matures them. But Catherine Earnshaw is obviously not realistic in any ordinary sense of the word. She may be attractive to students because of her romantic intensity of feeling, but it is pointless to apply ordinary common-sense psychology to her. A careful reading of the novel shows, indeed, that her behavior is contrasted with that of Mr. Lockwood, whose conventional realistic notion of Catherine and Heathcliff is made to look absurd.

One of the important things that needs to be done when students draw out their measuring sticks labeled "realism" is to force some consideration of what that word really means, and, for that matter, what the word "ordinary" means when one talks about ordinary experience. Obviously, in a minute or two of such discussion chaos will be enthroned. Students should be made to see that a comment like "But I know people like that" can be made to turn the most exaggerated sort of experience in the novel into realism. There undoubtedly were, for example, one-legged sea-captains like Captain Ahab. There is no reason why one such sea-captain might not have taken it into his head to get even with a whale that made him lose his leg. For the student, the notion of realism should be related to the notion of probability and circumstantial detail.

It would be a mistake to go much beyond that in class. It would be impossible to define "realistic" satisfactorily, either in class or out, without wandering over arid and obscure deserts of philosophy. The idea of "realism" in the novel ought to be arbitrarily defined in terms of certain conventions recognizable in fiction. These conventions usually do determine our response to particular works, and certainly help us decide whether there is any point in trying to understand them according to the standards of ordinary common sense and experience. Crudely, realistic novels are novels which (1) attend in detail to the surface of experience—the clothes a character wears, his complexion, his figure; the furniture, the houses, and so on; (2) treat characters as social beings, having a clearly defined place in society or seeking for one; (3) attend to the social surroundings and the interplay between character and society; (4) sometimes, but not necessarily, attend to the detailed workings of a character's mind; (5) treat characters not as simple but as complex, not as embodiments of one or two major qualities, but as rounded and complicated human beings; (6) do not seem to place more importance on symbolic or allegorical import than on the details themselves. That this definition is crude is evident, but it is a beginning and works in helping us find ways of handling *Pride and Prejudice* or *Great Expectations* in ways different from *Moby Dick* and *Wuthering Heights*. On the other hand, it does not do much to help us distinguish *Pride and Prejudice* from *Great Expectations*, which, though it does seem to be realistic, has so many elements of fairy tale and grotesquerie in it that it comes from a world different from that of Jane Austen's novel.

When we talk about "the novel" in the abstract, we tend to mean prose works which fall into the realistic tradition, and which tend to stress fidelity to experience at least as much as pattern, and character even more than plot. But there is another important tradition, which is less modern than the realistic novel and which critics tend to call romance. *The Scarlet Letter* or *Moby Dick* or *Wuthering Heights*, although they all partake of some of the qualities of the realistic novel, are basically romances. Almost all novel-romances will be found to have elements of realism in them, but they tend to have the following characteristics: (1) a sharply defined pattern, both in the development of plot and in the relation of characters; (2) a tendency to idealize characters, to make them either profoundly good or profoundly evil, or to treat them as the embodiments of single qualities, almost in the manner of allegory; (3) a tendency to sacrifice the development of character to the development of plot; (4) a consequent tendency toward a transcendence of normal human feelings for almost demonic emotional intensity; (5) a disregard of most surface detail; and (6) a symbolic or allegorical treatment of experience. It is important always to work under the assumption that there are no pure romances or pure realistic novels; and although these characteristics should warn us that we need to have our students treat *Wuthering Heights*, say, very differently from the way they would treat *Great Expectations*, they might also help students to see that Miss Havisham belongs to a world like that of *Wuthering Heights*, and Mr. Lockwood belongs to a world like that of *Great Expectations*.

It should be noted that one of the most distinguished modern critics, Northrop Frye (who, by the way, would argue that the novel is the last, not the first, form to be studied) notes two other kinds of novels besides those belonging to the conventions of realism and romance. He discusses the "confession" and the "satire." But the confession, which is related to autobiography, can easily be seen to belong to the conventions of realism. Take, for example, *The Mill on the Floss*. That novel, now out of favor because of the blight of *Silas Marner*—misused for generations—would make a fine book for serious study by superior high school students. Clearly, it is in large part fictionalized autobiography of George Eliot herself. It is a book which, like most "confessions," is deeply concerned with ideas; but by and large it is about man in society, and its treatment of Maggie Tulliver is precisely in the realistic tradition. *David Copperfield* is a slightly different matter, since the treatment of character in that book is only partially within the rounded and unallegorical tradition of the realistic novel. But the problem with that book is no different from that with any book which combines elements of realism and romance. Similarly, satire usually can be set crudely within the traditions of romance or realism. *The Way of All Flesh*, though it is largely satirical and deeply concerned with ideas, is fundamentally within the tradition of realism. *Brave New World*, though it makes a show of realism, lies largely within the tradition of romance. Crudely speaking, then, one might say that the further a novel pushes in the direction of discussion of abstract ideas, the closer it comes to romance and the more thoroughly the teacher will have to move away from considerations of character and the application of realistic standards.

There are, of course, many other kinds of "novel," but it seems to me that almost all of them might be regarded as sub-kinds of either realistic novel or romance. The modern tendency from Henry James to Joyce and Hemingway is to use realistic conventions within novels which in effect are romances, as for example, *The Portrait of a Lady, Ulysses,* and *The Old Man and the Sea.* But the enormous differences among these three novels ought to suggest how widely divergent novels are in kind, and how carefully a teacher must avoid applying any single "method." It seems to me then that one of the major tasks of the teacher is not to impose any arbitrary definitions on his students, but to channel the students' instinctive responses to the particular novels under discussion so that they will see the distinctive quality of each novel and will acquire the flexibility in reading which comes from a sensitivity to form.

I should like now to turn to a few of the elements that are likely to be found in novels of any kind, especially as they relate to form, and to suggest how one might move in class from one element to the other until the major questions about a novel are asked, and at least some of them are answered. And despite the distinctions I have been making so far, I see no harm in making as one's starting point the student's natural inclination to use a realistic standard for all novels. There is no point in discouraging the student's natural and human impulse to find a direct relation between literature and life. What one has to do is prove to him that the best way to discover that relation is by understanding how a novel works and, particularly, what its form is. For this reason, it seems to me important that after making what concessions are necessary to the student's concern with the personality of characters, and after trying to show students whether realistic canons can in fact be applied to the characters, a teacher should try to move on to a consideration of the novel as a whole.

Once a student is forced to turn from problems of character and realism, the first question he is likely to ask is, "What does the book mean?" Again, the instinct is sound; unfortunately, the kind of answer he is likely to want is something that no book ought to be able to supply. What he wants is a sentence which points the moral, such as, "Pride causes prejudice, and you must be willing to give up pride and look beneath the surface of things." Or, "One must not rely on good fortune or great hopes but rather work hard and honestly." Even for romances, which tend to move in the direction of abstract moral notions, this sort of answer, especially coming early in the discussion of a novel, is the worst possible sort if the teacher wants the student to get to know the book and to experience literature fully. It leads to the substitution of an idea for the book. Moreover, even when not inaccurate, such sentences could never encompass the full meaning of any good book, because such moral platitudes have meaning only if they are connected to and qualified by experience.

It is important, as one moves gingerly toward meaning, to try to show that the book has not one theme but many and that the full meaning of the book can be understood only by first understanding what the many themes are, as they seem to grow from the characters and action, and how they relate to each other. But it is best to pause here to work out a usable definition of "theme."

To begin with, a theme is not a moral. A theme is an idea, frequently not completely worked out so as to be stateable in a sentence, which grows out of the text and tends to be repeated with variations and developed as the novel progresses. A theme can take the shape of a single word—say, "pride"—, or of a phrase—"the difference between appearance and reality"—, or of a sentence—"all men have within them the capacity for great good or great evil." As a novel progresses, the various themes which at first need to be talked of as single words or phrases may be developed so as to be treatable as part of a sentence, as, for example, "Pride tends to prejudice (another theme) and to the mistaking of appearances for reality." But even such a sentence as this is obviously incomplete, and needs to be brought together with a great many other themes, all duly qualified and expanded by the experience of the novel. But if theme as word or sentence is meaningless without the experience behind it, it is nevertheless important because once a student begins to notice how one and then many themes can be seen to grow out of the characters and the action, he can also begin to see that there is such a thing as form, and that the form of the book is not only closely related to the meaning of it, but part of its meaning.

The problem of form is a particularly ticklish one, first because it is the one the students are least interested in, and second because, in relation to the novel at least, it is so ill-defined a notion. There are many ways in which a novel can be given form, and I should like here to note a few of them.

(1) The most obvious kind of form for a student to recognize is the form that grows from development of character. When he reads *The Red Badge of Courage*, for example, he necessarily becomes aware of the dramatic shift in the hero's behavior and in his attitude toward war. He may not fully understand the causes or recognize the full nature of the change, but he can see that all the events of the story focus on the hero and have their effects on him; and even if the student is initially far more absorbed in the excitement of the war than in the changes in the hero's character, it will not seem to him stretching things if one tries to show that the progress of the book is the progress of Henry Fleming's character.

(2) Plot is another obvious kind of form. If the book moves through a series of incidents in the direction of some sort of climax and then resolution of the conflicts which give it its drama, it has at least some rudimentary form. Sometimes the pattern which emerges from the plot is obviously symmetrical and clear. So, for

example, we can see how the first half of *Pride and Prejudice* shows Elizabeth Bennett's increasing misunderstanding of Darcy, and the second half moves us irrevocably toward the dispersal of misunderstanding and the joys of marriage. In Conrad's *The Secret Sharer* we have a less obvious pattern, but one that is clear enough. It is the form of the conventional thriller: the beginnings in mystery, concealment, and adventure which build the suspense toward the climactic escape. But as soon as we recognize that the book's pattern follows a tightly conceived plot, we realize that the plot is determined by other elements. For example, the plot of *Pride and Prejudice* is determined in part by the problem of growth of character, in part by the themes which give the book its name. Indeed, the form supplied by plot does not by itself carry us far in an approach to the meaning of the book.

If the student is allowed to think of the plot of a novel in the abstract, without close reference to the way it unfolds in the novel, he is likely to get a misleading idea of what the book is up to. He needs, for example, to be made alert to the crude but famous distinction between scenic and panoramic presentation. When, for example, a novel summarizes a good deal of action and compresses long periods of time into a few paragraphs or into a chapter or so, its presentation is panoramic. And in all likelihood that kind of presentation implies that the author is only conducting some necessary business, important largely as it moves his book closer to the really important actions, which will almost always be presented as scenes. A scene will, of course, cover a very short period of time, and represent the action dramatically, usually with dialogue. When a scene is presented in great detail, the student should be alerted to the likelihood that in it important things about character, plot, and meaning are being developed.

The distinction between scene and panorama is related to an even more important and general distinction—that between what might be called "description" and "dramatization." The student should be reminded persistently that what makes a book valuable and convincing is not an author's general assertion that character A is kind and intelligent and character B is vicious and stupid, but his demonstration by showing how characters think, talk, and behave that they are such and such kind of people. Inevitably, if an author is any good, he will demonstrate simply through dramatization that general labels like "good" and "bad" are inadequate to a description of human behavior. The attractiveness of such labels is one of the greatest impediments to adequate appreciation of a novel. The student must be forced, by whatever tricks the teacher can devise, to surrender his moral prejudices as he reads. If a character does a "bad" thing, the student is likely to lose all sympathy for him (or assume he should lose it). Labels and experience don't mix. And one of the best ways to indicate the moral complexity of experience is to turn to the problem of point of view.

(3) Point of view is another element that determines form. This is the form that is imposed on a novel by the mind of the character through whom the action is viewed, or by the mind of the author himself as he chooses to reveal or not to reveal certain relevant information. It shouldn't be too difficult to show about *Pride and Prejudice*, for instance, that the plot as we have it now would be very weak, though just as symmetrical and clear, if we were allowed by the author confidently to see more than Elizabeth Bennett herself can see. Again, in *The Secret Sharer*, the adventure would remain if the story weren't told from the point of view of the captain. But the point of view forces on our attention that the adventure of the external plot is secondary to the adventure of the captain's mind. The student should be made aware of how thoroughly dependent we are on what the author chooses to let us know at any given moment. The revelation of a fact too early or too late might destroy the effect of an entire work.

Discussion in class of point of view in general is probably pointless unless there is time for a good deal of confusion. The standard division between first and third person or omniscient and limited points of view is altogether inadequate to describe the enormous variety of perspectives from which the action of a novel can be observed. To take two examples to which I will refer again later, *Great Expectations* and *Wuthering Heights*, though novels of apparently simple construction, are narrated from very complicated points of view. *Great Expectations* is, by and large, seen through the eyes of Pip, but it is Pip as a grown man who narrates the story. The novel thus partakes of the qualities of both first and third person narrations, since Pip records the experience as he felt it as a child and at the same time he looks back on himself and even moralizes on his actions like a detached observer. He gives a sense of immediacy and withholds information which would give the important secrets away; at the same time, he tells more about the experience and the meaning of experience than the young Pip could possibly have known. In *Wuthering Heights*, of course, there is a great variety of perspectives on the action. We have Lockwood's view of the experience, which is gradually clarified by Nelly Dean's narrative. Neither of these characters is capable of understanding the characters and action they describe. Moreover, there is a combination of immediate record of experience which is in the process of unfolding, and retrospective narration. Thus, it is possible to say that the point of view in both books is "limited," but what is important is to show precisely in what way it is limited and what effect the limitations have on the novels as wholes.

(4) A novel can acquire form from repetitions and parallels. In *Pride and Prejudice*, the misunderstandings between Elizabeth and Darcy parallel the breakup between Jane Bennett and Mr. Bingley. In *The Secret Sharer*, the single plot line gains its strength from the way we are allowed to see that the story of the captain is a perfect parallel to that of Leggatt; and the excitement of the external plot—whether Leggatt will escape—is paralleled by the more important excitement—whether the captain's fate at his crisis will be the same as Leggatt's fate at his. Moreover, students should always be alerted to parallels and repetitions on a much smaller scale: for example, the repetition of words, the reappearance of

objects, the reoccurrence of figures of speech. The square finger Mr. Gradgrind points at the class in the first chapter of *Hard Times* is made important by Dickens' repetition of the word "square" and his association of squareness with facts, an association which continues throughout the novel. In reading *The Lord of the Flies*, any student can be made to see that Piggy's glasses, and the conch, and the fire, have an importance which raises them to the level of symbol and relates them to theme. Where a novel tends to repeat certain kinds of actions, or characters, or words, or images, there is likely to be a significance which a student should be equipped to recognize.

(5) All of these various kinds of form might appear in a single work, and all can be subsumed under two general notions of form. The first is the notion of form as relation. That is, we can work out the form of a novel when we can answer the question about anything in it, "What is its relation to the novel as a whole?" The question usually can be put another way: "Why does this happen here?" Once a student has got used to the idea that a novelist plans his book so that certain characters will be like other characters, certain actions are similar to certain other actions, certain facts are withheld in one place and given in another, he will be ready (if not eager) for such questions. One should be able to ask a student, for example, why *All the King's Men* doesn't begin at the beginning but rather with the scene in which Jack Burden, Willie Stark, and Sugar Boy are hurtling down the highway in a great black limousine. They should be made to see that there are a good many reasons—for example: to introduce us to Willie's work (the highway was constructed by him); to introduce the theme of change and rapidity of motion and mortality which becomes so important in the novel and which is the central fact of Jack's life; to lead us into the story at its central moment, when Jack's quest for his father begins in earnest even though he isn't aware of it; to show us the major qualities of Willie Stark—the modern man, builder of highways and exploiter of power—and especially, his use

of his insight into the fallen nature of man, which will become the means by which Jack discovers his father and reenters the world. And so on. Or, to take an example less obvious and important, why, in *The Red Badge of Courage*, at an early stage of the fighting, does Crane say not that the men were shot and killed but only that "The men dropped here and there like bundles"? Questions like this, chosen randomly, can lead students into discussion of the most important aspects of the novel and can do so while showing them that novels are composed of language, that they are not mere records of experience but conscious manipulations of it, that the language creates the story, and that everything in the novel is related to everything else.

(6) The other general notion of form under which all the others might be subsumed is the notion of form as theme. The plots of novels generally are unfolded so as to impose some sort of form on experience, which in its raw state is chaotic and meaningless. We have seen already that the form of the plot of *Pride and Prejudice* is related to its major concerns about human behavior. Equally, the plot of *The Secret Sharer* becomes a kind of paradigm of human experience, and becomes meaningful only when it is seen to reflect certain universal facts about the way people are tested by experience and the way they are all within a hair's breadth of defeat, and so on. It may be that certain things in a novel have no apparent relevance to the plot or to development of character, but are nevertheless important for the novel as a whole. If this be the case, it will usually be found that the apparent irrelevancies can be explained as thematically relevant. What, for example, is the whole long episode about Cass Mastern and the pre-Civil-War South doing in *All the King's Men*? The episode certainly does not further the plot as far as its length would seem to require, and it does not develop Jack's character much. We discover that Cass's story and his relation to his brother is meant to be a parallel to Jack's story and his relation to Willie; but we see immediately that the full scope of the episode develops certain themes: among them, that

our virtues are the defects of our vices, our vices the defects of our virtues; that purity is impossible in this changing world; that we must all assume a burden of guilt; that power need not be evil and is frequently less evil than absolute virtue.

Equally important, we need to keep in mind that elements which contribute to the other kinds of form I have mentioned contribute as well to thematic form. Students should never be given large doses of pure form; form should be tied to meaning as much as possible, especially since in the novel, with no long traditions to give it shape, meaning is almost inevitably form itself. The student must be made to remember that if he wants to find a "moral" or he wants to understand character, he can do it only by facing problems of form, as for example, the problem of point of view in *Pride and Prejudice.* Only by seeing how the limitations of Elizabeth's vision, which grow out of her pride, keep her from learning the truth about Darcy, can one move successfully out to such comforting themes as, "It is important not to allow vanity to get in the way of one's recognition of other people's motives and behavior."

Having been made aware that every work has a form of its own, the student can be made to see that in every work he is being given not a piece of life itself, but a personal vision of life. The word "vision" is an important one, because although it implies the imposition of a pattern on experience and therefore an attempt to make experience meaningful, it does not imply a summary of experience in a few easily held aphorisms. Rather, it implies a way of seeing which gives experience a personal coherence not logical but deeply felt as valid. The form is the expression of the vision. Thus, if we look at almost any novel by Dickens, we find that practically everything in it is seen with the exaggeration of a child's response and that it is held together by an extraordinary series of apparent coincidences. The exaggeration and the coincidences imply that the world is full of mystery, excitement, terror, and joy, and that somehow there are forces operating in it which extend beyond the powers of man's influence. This holds true whatever the particular themes of the individual novels may be, and to bring this to the attention of students will be to make it possible for them to judge the novel on its own terms. They can then, of course, go beyond the text itself and compare its vision with their own sense of the world; but they should be better prepared to judge the novel by their own standards. Instead of saying, "Is this the way the world really is?" they might be brought to ask the far more fruitful question, "Are there any elements in experience which might justify Dickens' vision, even if that vision is only partial?"

The process I recommend in the studying of novels in class, then, is a movement from the immediate and crude application of experience to the novel, to a consideration of the form of each novel in its own right, to a final and reconsidered application of experience to the vision which the form and substance of the novel evokes. I have avoided going into much detail here about the usual subjects of "conflicts," "drama," and so on because it seems to me that these are the kinds of things that students themselves respond to instinctively, if they are going to respond to literature at all. The teacher can talk about these things as they emerge in their appropriate places in the discussion of form and vision.

But the real problem in teaching the novel is to find a way to talk about meaning which does justice to the size and complexity and detail of the works, and particularly to break through the student's tendency to see the novel as something that just "growed." If he can be made to see that the author is manipulating material even in the most straightforward, chronologically direct of novels, he can begin to move beyond the superficial notions of realism which he has, not quite articulated, in his head, and can begin to see more precisely the kind of relation the novel has to life. It is not merely a mirror of what the student already knows, it is a perception of experience in any of various ways which ought to move the student beyond his own experience, and to make him see that the artist uses experience not to reestablish already established conventions of seeing and judging, but to break them down. The form he gives to experience in the novel is his commentary on the old ways (which generally mean the student's ways, among others), and if the student is looking for morals he is likely to find more than he bargained for if he can be made to face a great novel on its own terms.

ON TEACHING *Great Expectations*

It might be useful, given the wide variety of forms and kinds one can find in works conventionally called novels, to consider two novels and suggest ways in which discussion of them ought to differ accordingly as they waver between pure "romance" and pure "realistic" novel. There are many novels more obviously different from each other than *Great Expectations* and *Wuthering Heights*, but I think it useful to note how strikingly different in kind two works can be, although they are products of the same culture and although they both can be described as works which distinctly mingle the forms of realistic novel and romance.

Like any good popular entertainment—like television drama to-day—*Great Expectations* combines an intense realism with elements of fairy tale. But for the most part, the story is a realistic one, centering very carefully on Pip, who is created as a fully rounded character, and who changes and develops as the story progresses. In its portrayal of Pip, his growth, and his relationships with his society, *Great Expectations* unquestionably falls within the realistic conventions I have described. We are required to understand his behavior in literal, not symbolic or allegorical ways. And if the story has a moral—it has, in fact, many morals—, it grows out of a richly imagined experience, which, though highly patterned, is subservient to the development of Pip's character and which, except for a few lurid moments, as, for example, those in which Orlick threatens to burn Pip in the kiln, remains largely within the emotional range of ordinary human activity.

A classroom study of *Great Expectations* ought certainly to take advantage of the popular-realistic nature of Dickens' art in that novel by focusing on Pip's character. This emphasis has the virtue of leading directly into the essential problems of the novel and its essential form, because Pip is both main actor and narrator. Everything that happens is seen from his point of view, and the book is fundamentally "about" what he learns from his own experience. Moreover, Dickens is particularly careful to awaken sympathy for Pip from the start, although he tries also to impress the reader through Pip's own words and actions with Pip's guilt. And this sympathy never dissipates although it is modified.

Character, in *Great Expectations*, is one of the most important aspects of its form, and one might usefully exploit a class's responses to Pip the character in order to show this. First, one might ask, why is Pip so sympathetic a figure at the outset? For one thing, he *is* a mere pip, an entirely insignificant speck, about whom we immediately learn that he is without family, his mother, father, and "five little brothers" having died before him. His first conscious moment is of himself as a "small bundle of shivers growing afraid of it all and beginning to cry" (ch. I), and then of the threatening and terrifying convict. His earliest years are spent being "brought up by hand" (that is, like a calf taken from its mother's milk, farmed out) by a shrewish sister who drops pins in his bread and makes him feel guilty for being alive. Here are all the elements of melodrama—the full exploitation of natural human sympathy for the innocent, the helpless, and the maltreated.

The first eight chapters of the first book intensify and develop this aspect of Pip's character. And despite their partly melodramatic quality, these chapters are scrupulously careful about the surface details of experience and about making Pip seem like a real boy in a real—and harsh—world. We are made to feel that just as he has no parents, and as his sister makes him think himself a burden and unwanted, so he is completely cut off from the respectable society represented by his sister, Mr. Wopsle, Mr. and Mrs. Hubble, and especially the hypocrite, Uncle Pumblechook.

And as Miss Havisham and Estella enter the story, it becomes clear that one of Pip's major problems will be to establish some sort of meaningful relation with the society in which he begins as an outcast.

The next stage in the growth of Pip's character is clear. Although Estella—and especially Miss Havisham—are figures out of gothic fiction, the latter being a kind of bad fairy, their effect on Pip is meant to have an entirely realistic psychological explanation. (Moreover, in keeping with the basically realistic conventions in which the book works, we shall see that both Estella and Miss Havisham become in the later stages of the book not mere evil influences but human beings whose behavior is meant to be psychologically explicable.) They lead Pip into the second stage of development, where the consciousness of feeling is replaced by the consciousness of intellect and convention so that Pip begins to deserve the guilt which, as a helpless and abused innocent, he had originally so unjustifiably felt. As he grows into full consciousness he grows away from the life of feeling, embodied in the figures of Joe Gargery, who is all heart and barely any head at all, and Biddy. Whereas Joe leads Pip to feel sympathy for all outcasts, even for the convict, whom he calls a "poor miserable fellow creature" (ch. V), Estella leads Pip to be ashamed of his dirty hands and his clumsy looks and eventually to be repelled not only by the convict but by Joe himself.

This second stage of Pip's development as a character is explored fully in the second section of the book, presided over in Pip's mind by the evil genius of Miss Havisham and Stella. In London, with his unexpected and misunderstood wealth, Pip increasingly incurs the guilt of ingratitude as he cuts off Joe and Biddy, and recklessly spends his money in the futile hope of winning Estella. Our sympathy for him is sustained in two ways: first, by Pip's own recognition of his ingratitude and by his guilt, and second, by the fact that Pip, the narrator, has clearly come through all this experience as a better man. Moreover, in his relations with Herbert Pocket and Mr. Wemmick, Pip remains essentially good-natured and loving.

The third stage of Pip's development corresponds, of course, to the third stage of the novel as a whole, and to the third book. In that book, Pip begins to make the discoveries which show him that the values into which Estella and Miss Havisham led him are altogether inferior to the values of Joe, and he therefore begins to move in the direction of his lost innocence. But of course innocence once lost can never, by definition, be regained. And thus he turns back to Biddy too late and, though Joe nurses him through his illness, he can never return to Joe for long, since the past—though it has not altered Joe's feelings—has made Pip too keenly aware of his own moral inferiority.

Tracing this simple literal level of Pip's personal journey through the novel and the development of his personality clearly leads to a visible pattern for the book as a whole: from innocence, to guilt, to redemption. Moreover, as soon as one recognizes this pattern in Pip's life, the triadic structure of the book in many other aspects can be made clear. For example, the book opens in the country, where innocence is possible, moves to the city, where man has defaced nature, and Pip's moral recovery is indicated by his visit to the country once again (ch. XLVIII). (But of course, Paradise once lost cannot be regained, and Pip returns to work, though not in the city but in the "East.") Equally, Pip's relations with Joe fall into the pattern marked out by innocence, guilt and redemption, as do his relations with Magwitch. Each relationship suggests the primacy of love and the need for suffering, for the purging away of pride, great expectations, and guilt; each reenacts the basic Christian pattern in the person of an ordinary boy with ordinary human failings so that the realistic development of his character moves into the area of symbol.

Thus, one moves from plot and character to theme with little difficulty. Pip's innocence at the start of the novel is combined with a) his alienation from respectable society; b) his morality of

instinctive love and sympathy; c) his heedlessness of intellect and
convention; d) his loyalty to Joe and Biddy; e) his acceptance of
his own lot and his willingness to work and earn his right to live;
f) his humility; g) his exaggerated and almost caricatured perception of experience so that everything seems large and wonderful
or terrifying to him. But as he is influenced by Stella, each one
of these things changes. He aspires to respectable society and to
be a gentleman; he deliberately subdues his instinctive sympathy
and love in favor of what is practical and conventional (as in his
farewell to Biddy and his treatment of Joe on Joe's visit to his London apartment); he stops working and relies not on his own powers
but on the hoped-for reality of his great expectations; he becomes
proud and largely cynical. We can infer from these aspects of
innocence and experience most of the major ideas of the novel:
the dignity of the innocent and poor, the primacy of instinct over
convention and intelligence, the dependence of the powerful on
the weak, and so on.

The working out of the plot in the final section of the book can
be seen on this thematic level as a purgation of all the sins of
experience and convention and a return, as close as possible, to
the state of innocence. The fact that it has been Magwitch, not
Miss Havisham, who gave him the money makes clear how
spurious and absurd the notion of respectability is, since a gentleman's money always comes up from the dirt, in one way or other;
he learns from Magwitch the morality of instinctive love, as opposed to pragmatic morality, and in his loving effort to help his
benefactor escape and then to stay with Magwitch until he dies,
he redeems himself of his disloyalty and fall from innocent love;
his experience with the maddened and jealous Orlick is a kind of
mirror-image of his own worst self, and he learns—in his near
escape from death—not only the viciousness of living one's life on
the basis of great expectations as opposed to hard work and earned
merit, but the importance of humility and of moderation of one's
demands upon life. He pierces, for the first time, beneath the veil

of appearances to the moral reality of the respectable and decorous world.

Just as analysis of character and plot can lead to these larger considerations of the major themes of the novel, so too can a consideration of the plot in general and the point of view from which it is narrated. The plot itself is a dramatic embodiment of the themes, and the plot would have been entirely different even if the events had been the same, had the point of view been different. The plot is one of the most immediately attractive aspects of the novel to the student, since it depends so heavily on the unraveling of certain mysteries: who is Pip's benefactor, who is Jaggers' servant, why does Miss Havisham behave as she does, will Pip marry Stella, and what is the meaning of the strange flash of recognition Pip sometimes feels as he looks at Stella. The unraveling of the story moves directly to theme because it turns out that both Pip's money and Pip's love are tainted by the prison which, from his early youth, Pip did everything he could to ignore —though he felt the taint. We come back again to the pervasive theme that the respectable superstructure of society rests on an underworld of outcasts so that the mere conventions of the gentleman are absurd and hypocritical. What should govern society is not decorum and legal precision (as in Jaggers and half the time in Wemmick) but love. If anyone should genuinely know this, it is of course Pip the outcast. But in order to know it fully, Pip must become one of the respectable, one of the hypocrites, one of the oppressors. He must lose his innocence to find it again in experience.

But the impact of the story depends on the point of view from which it is told. If we knew from the start that Magwitch was Pip's benefactor and that Stella was born in prison, the daughter of Magwitch and Jaggers' servant, and that Miss Havisham was jilted by Magwitch's enemy, we could not feel what it means to be trapped by the illusions of respectability. We must be made to feel what Pip feels, and so the narrator—though he knows how the story will come out—only hints at possible solutions and in fact forces us to see the experience through the eyes of the young Pip. Here the theme of the disparity between the respectable and the real is embodied within the very method of narration.

Just as the values with which *Great Expectations* concludes are the firm, middle-class values of sympathy, hard work, humility, and success (both Herbert Pocket and Pip are ultimately fairly successful), so the novel rarely moves to the titanic emotional heights of tragedy, or of a romantic novel like *Wuthering Heights*. Miss Havisham, Pumblechook, Trabb's boy, Orlick, Jaggers, even to a certain extent, Wemmick are hardly rounded and realistic characters. But they all feed into the perceptions of rounded and realistic Pip, and they all live in immediately recognizable urban and country surroundings. They people a novel whose hyperrealistic exaggerations and emotional intensity all feed back into the moderate and soothing emotions of the middle class. They echo from the world of romance, but they are considerably more tamed than romantic characters. Indeed, they are romantic characters going realistic, and they are more recognizable as exaggerations of what goes on in life than as figures who break through the confines of recognizable experience into a world of their own.

ON TEACHING *Wuthering Heights*

If, in *Great Expectations*, the peripheral characters come out of romance to feed the realistic traditions of the novel proper, in *Wuthering Heights* the peripheral characters come out of realistic traditions to serve as a background to romance. They help remind us, by the inadequacy of their responses to the main characters, that conventional realistic standards of judgment cannot work on *Wuthering Heights*. Mr. Lockwood and Nelly Dean talk and act in conventional ways and bring to bear on the actions they watch precisely the middle-class morality which is the center of *Great Expectations*. But from the time Mr. Lockwood walks into Heathcliff's sullen household until, at the end, when he wonders as he looks at Catherine, Edgar, and Heathcliff's graves "how any one could ever imagine unquiet slumbers for the sleepers in that quiet earth," he totally misunderstands and misvalues the book's experience. *Wuthering Heights* remains somewhere between realistic novel and romance because the "real" world is a constant intruder on the emotionally intense world of the Earnshaws and Lintons; because the novel's perfectly symmetrical narrative pattern does not lead to a total de-emphasis of character; and because its abstractable moral notions are even less articulable than those of *Great Expectations.*

If one begins a study of *Wuthering Heights* with a consideration of the characters of Heathcliff, the two Catherines, and Hareton, as one might begin a study of *Great Expectations* with a study of Pip, one is likely to find that the book does not open up as one might expect. The formal pattern of the book emerges largely from the plot and the juxtaposition of characters rather than from the development of particular characters. The following diagram, constructed by C. P. Sanger in his extraordinary 1926 paper on "The Structure of *Wuthering Heights*," should serve to indicate how very carefully worked out the narrative balance is:

Mr. Earnshaw	m.	Mrs. Earnshaw			Mr. Linton	m.	Mrs. Linton
d. Oct.		d. Spring			d. Autumn		d. Autumn
1777		1773			1780		1780

Hindley	m.	Frances	Catherine	m.	Edgar	Heathcliff	m.	Isabella
b. Summer		d. late	b. Summer		b. 1762	b. 1764	Jan.	b. late
1757		1778	1765		d. Sept.	d. May	1784	1765
d. Sept.			d. Mar. 20,		1801	1802		d. June
1784			1784					1797

Hareton		m.		Catherine		m.		Linton
b. June	Jan. 1, 1803		b. Mar. 20,	Aug. 1801		b. Sept. 1784		
1778			1784			d. Oct. 1801		

The symmetry here, producing relationships more balanced than anything one is likely to find in life, suggests that we are not dealing with a realistic novel. Moreover, as one watches the details of these carefully balanced relationships, one notices how the Linton

family at Thrushcross Grange is symbolically balanced in its do-
mestic moderation against the Earnshaw family at Wuthering
Heights with its passionate denial of all moderation and "normal-
ity." Again, as further confirmation that *Wuthering Heights* is close
to a romance, one finds that where, in *Great Expectations,* Pip
grows and changes, Heathcliff and Catherine do not change at all.
Even at the end, when Heathcliff seems to relent, we find he has
not changed. Rather he has simply been drained of energy by the
obsession which he cannot resist: "I have a single wish," he says,
"and my whole being and faculties are yearning to attain it."
Moreover, where one can explain Pip's actions by reference to the
influences around him, his innocence, the ordinary temptations
that confront any human being, one finds that all of Heathcliff's
behavior is on a large scale—on a scale so large that it seems in
excess of any possible motive. Only in the world of the romance,
where emotions are almost elemental in intensity, is such behavior
explicable.

This doesn't mean, of course, that character should be ignored.
Clearly, the characters of Catherine and Heathcliff are the things
that most attract students, and they should be understood—but on
their own terms. Heathcliff, though he may be seen in part as the
orphan boy and alien who seeks revenge against the oppressive
ruling class, is more interesting as a timeless figure. He is a man
of preternatural emotional strength and intensity for whom the
life of feeling transcends all other considerations and who becomes
emotionally fused with Cathy so that the two regard each other
as one. The winning of Cathy and then vengeance for her loss are
the totality of Heathcliff's life, and against such intensity normal
moral reasoning is not only futile; it is absurd. Thus, when having
trapped Isabella Linton into marrying him, he is questioned by
Nelly Dean, Heathcliff responds, "I have no pity! I have no pity!
The more the worms writhe, the more I yearn to crush out their
entrails! It is a moral teething; and I grind with greater energy, in
proportion to the increase of pain." Nelly, almost comically, replies

in the language of the middle-class moralist: "Do you understand what the word pity means?" Heathcliff, rightly, doesn't even bother to answer since Nelly is speaking to him across an abyss of incomprehension.

Catherine, although she makes her compromise with the culture represented by the Lintons, is equally intense. Her destruction is not really the result of Heathcliff's persistence but of her compromise with her own nature in marrying Edgar Linton. Her nature—which like Heathcliff's does not change—is expressed clearly as she laments her fevered condition before her death: "Oh, I'm burning," she says, "I wish I were out of doors! I wish I were a girl again, half savage and half hardy, and free . . . and laughing at injuries, not maddening under them . . . I'm sure I should be myself were I once among the heather on those hills. Open the window wide: fasten it open!" Catherine and Heathcliff are elemental forces like the wind on the Heights, and it is appropriate that our first knowledge of Catherine should come from the battering of wind against the window while Lockwood is sleeping in her room.

Just as one cannot get too far in an understanding of the book through study of character, so one can get almost nowhere by attempting to find a meaning reducible to a sentence or two. The absurdity of Nelly and Mr. Lockwood in the face of Heathcliff and Catherine should be sufficient warning that an attempt to draw a simple moral from the novel will break down. We have already seen that Heathcliff does not reform but, like some natural elements, simply wears down after a violent and impersonal career. That the novel ends with the happy ending of the conventional novel ought not to mislead the reader into thinking that the conclusion makes some sort of moral commentary on the brutality and egotism of Heathcliff and Catherine. The second Catherine and Hareton come together because they are less strong than the first Catherine and Heathcliff, not because they are morally superior. The symmetry of the plot to which I have already pointed is part of the key to the whole narrative. The events that take place are ultimately entirely impersonal, the result of natural affinities or antagonisms, not of subtle modifications of personality.

Thus, it is the plot itself which is the key to the meanings of *Wuthering Heights*. The Earnshaws struggle among themselves like animals; they devour the Lintons as beasts devour weaker animals; but the Lintons exercise an influence on Catherine in the way cat-lovers can win a cat by offering it certain kinds of comforts impossible in the impersonal world of beasts. They cannot, however, expunge from the cat its animal instincts. The softening between Catherine Linton and Hareton is a result of the fact that the second Catherine has Linton as well as Earnshaw blood in her and also that Hareton has assimilated some of Heathcliff's temperament while Catherine has of course much of her mother in her.

In other words, explanations must remain on the elemental, not the psychological, realistic, or moral levels. They emerge from the facts of the plot rather than from modifications in the characters. Nelly Dean's constant attempts to influence behavior by means of conventional moral judgments not only fail, but usually serve to make matters worse. As the story reaches us, filtered through the eyes of Nelly Dean and Lockwood, we become aware that neither of these two can offer an adequate explanation of the experience.

The greatest danger to be avoided as one discusses *Wuthering Heights* in class is the tendency to moralize the characters. One ought to exploit the natural sympathy the students feel with Heathcliff and Catherine to help them avoid their trained response to regard everything in easy moral terms. Perhaps the question to ask the students directly is how they can reconcile their admiration of these two characters with the almost total immorality or amorality of their actions. Their instinctive sympathy with Heathcliff in his love of Catherine and his hatred of Edgar Linton and Hindley Earnshaw is clearly part of the intention of the novel.

Students will be forced then to recognize that there are certain things that they admire which are in conventional terms morally reprehensible and that it is not possible to talk about all things in moral terms. This is one of the key lessons of *Wuthering Heights,* and it is perhaps the most difficult to learn. *Wuthering Heights* is a novel about aspects of our experience which lie below the levels of social living and conscious control. Read correctly, it will challenge all our conventional notions of the relation of moral codes to behavior, and force upon students and teachers alike an illumination of their own experience and the elements of the impersonal in themselves. It has no moral.

3

On Teaching Short Stories

MARY ALICE BURGAN

Assistant Professor of English,
Indiana University

All literary criticism presupposes a concern with the relevance of
literature to life; it implies the question, "What difference does
literature make?" All of us who teach literature, it seems to me,
hope to open that question with our students in some degree on
whatever level we find them. The short story has special qualities
which can help us in this endeavor, and I would like to explore
some of those qualities here. How, then, does the short story help
us to initiate that question which asks about the difference which
literature makes? And how can a study of short fiction lead to
othor important questions about the relation of the various aspects
of a narrative to its whole?

The beginning of an answer lies in the fact that the short story
is immediately interesting. Usually it is "realistic," and usually its
setting is the modern world which the student knows. And the
modernity of the short story as a form which has only recently
been accepted in its own right not only makes it interesting, but
makes it interesting in a certain way. There are probably many
reasons why the modern writer began to take short fiction seriously as a genre—I am sure that the demands of periodicals like
The New Yorker have had a crucial effect on the prevalence of
the short story in our time—but, most importantly, the form has

provided a framework for the kind of vision which modern writers have of modern man.

We are all relatively familiar with the idea that the most important experiences of life occur on the inside; heroic action, painted on a grand scale, is interesting to us only so long as it gives us intimations of how the hero's inner action goes. The short story writer takes it for granted that we are suspicious of heroes anyway. He assumes that we are convinced that the world is made up of anonymous, unheroic people—like ourselves—who achieve the most momentous revelations of their lives in seemingly trivial and accidental occurrences. He seeks to heighten our sense that life is short and that character is nevertheless endlessly repetitive; he believes that fiction must capture both these facts in order to give us back that commanding and convincing image of ourselves which has always been one of the primary aims of art.

In his study of the short story, *The Lonely Voice*, Frank O'Connor has theorized the source of the short story's image of modern man may be related to its origins in countries like Russia, Ireland, and the United States, where there has existed historically a "submerged population" made up of the anonymous individuals who have been cut off from the established society of the majority. He believes that the novel—the English novel in particular—is centrally interested in man in society; the short story, on the other hand, places its character (and note that the word is in the singular) outside society and speaks of him and for him there. "As a result there is in the short story at its most characteristic something we do not often find in the novel—an intense awareness of human loneliness." Such a hypothesis about the essential nature of the short story does not pretend to be completely definitive, but it is suggestive. For example, it can enable us to point to the possible sources in the writer's angle of vision which cause the genre to assume the dimensions it ordinarily has. Thus it can help us to begin a discussion about literature in which we can guide the student to see that the interest in a story lies not only in its evocation of a familiar and recognizable world, but in the way it interprets that world.

We might ask a class to consider a familiar kind of story, say, the interminable soap opera. And we might note that the need for its tales to go on and on frequently determines their content: they must have characters whose problems are so involved that they can be unwound only by eternal discussion; there must be large families of mixed-up people in them to provide for shifts of interest; and the turns of plot must rest upon such catastrophes as murder, illegitimacy, divorce, nervous breakdown, and blackmail in order to carry on for fifteen minutes every day. But whose angle of vision do these tales fit? No single authorial intelligence seems to be guiding them. They are written by their audiences, for the vision to which they conform is the vision of the housewife who is at home alone, where nothing exciting ever happens and where she must daydream over her ironing board of another kind of world enough like her own to seem relevant, but replete with glamorous troubles which, let it be noted, are usually solved by a strong, housewifely heroine. Such an image may become hypnotic, but it is important to see that because it lacks any forming principle other than convention, it may also become very boring.

For balance I would add a short discussion of the fairy tale and the kind of image of man's life which it gives. I would note that the fairy tale frequently has as its hero an outcast, lonely man, but that that man usually triumphs. He wins the girl in the end, and he becomes king, and everyone lives happily ever after. But he achieves this glorious and exhilarating victory only because the hope and the desire which inform the fairy tale are so intense that they enable the story to take off from the everyday world and to suspend its rules. In the short story, life goes on as it always has; instead of seeing the possibility of triumph over great odds in it, we see ordinary life itself more clearly, and in rare cases, we understand the temptations and limited victories which it can hold for the isolated, unmagical encounter with experience.

One of the most famous cases of the lonely man in America is delineated in "The Secret Life of Walter Mitty." There are óther stories which might serve as well for an initial exploration of the special kind of interest inherent in the short story—Galsworthy's "Quality," Frank O'Connor's "The First Confession," or Hemingway's "Old Man at the Bridge" come to mind as alternatives. If the theory of the lonely man is adequate, any story should do, but I recommend starting with one which is short enough to be discussed in one class hour and which works in a conventionally realistic mode. "The Secret Life of Walter Mitty" has a familiar setting—an automobile on its way to town, a parking lot, a city street, a hotel lobby, and the sidewalk outside a drugstore. Above all, however, its central character is a clear charter member of a well-known "submerged population," that of the domesticated American male. We might refer the class to television again, asking students to remember the way the American male is depicted in family comedies. He is usually either a bumbling idiot, a Dagwood type, or he is too young and muscular and handsome and wise to be believed.

I think that it is unwise to linger on amateur sociologizing any longer than necessary to set up the frame of reference for a particular work. "The Secret Life of Walter Mitty" establishes its own framework very soon, and we don't want to mar that achievement by "typing" the central character in such a way that we will miss his particularity in the story. One way to get at this particularity might be to ask the class what kind of man Walter Mitty is in his daydreams. In the first dream, a pattern is initiated. He is a loner; he takes his own counsel. " 'I'm not asking you, Lieutenant Berg,' said the Commander. 'Throw on the power lights! Rev her up to 8,500! We're going through!' " His actions in the other dreams have the same quality of mysterious competency; on the surface they seem stupid, but in the final victory they reveal his cleverness, daring, and power. He asks for a fountain pen when the anesthetizer gives way in his operating room dream; he perversely reveals in the courtroom dream all the details which might convict him; he will fly alone in the war dream; and, of course, he is alone at the end, facing a firing squad with an insolent smile. This pattern should be easy to establish, and surely the process will take the class back to the story to see that the dreams are not random parodies of movie versions of heroism. Most students will begin to see the merely verbal clues from external events which inspire each fantasy, but it is more important that they see the version of another self which the dreams begin to formulate. They dramatize the fact that the Walter Mitty who knows that he appears ineffectual to an outsider like his wife is comforting himself with the thought that misleading appearances are common to all uncommon men.

I am emphasizing the pattern which the daydreams take here because in my own teaching of this story I have noted a tendency among students to dismiss them too simply as entertaining satires on the common man's escape mechanisms. They will read Walter Mitty as the hen-pecked husband type and let him go at that. I think they need to be led to see that the story takes him a little deeper. This can become even more apparent when they begin to connect the daydream world with the real one in which Walter Mitty lives. Mrs. Mitty seems to be the major force in that world, and she will obviously have to be treated in a discussion of the story. Again, I would make a stand against any tendency to categorize her merely as a nagging wife. I would look at the kinds of things she nags about—driving too fast, wearing rubbers, buying toothpaste, visiting the family doctor. In other words, it can be seen that her nagging implies its own version of what a normal man should be: he should be safe and clean and healthy. Now we can start to show that the world from which Walter Mitty finds himself outcast is the stable, social world where there is no virtue in man's striving beyond himself. The only admirable power must belong to the mindless young mechanics and their machines.

But students may become exasperated with Walter Mitty's subservience to his wife and his retreat to daydream. I have had students condemn him impatiently as a coward. I would counter this charge with an attempt to show the nobility of his character. Although his daydreams show him as an impulsive man, they also show him as a defender of the weak. There is triumph in these dreams, but there is no vindictiveness. Toward the end he does resist his wife momentarily, and it is pathetic that her last aggression sends him back to one more vision of grandeur, where he stands "erect and motionless, proud and disdainful, Walter Mitty the Undefeated, inscrutable to the last." But may we not perceive an invitation in this sentence to apply the final description of the hero to the everyday Walter Mitty as well as to the daydream one?

I do not think that an absolute answer can or should be given to that question, but we need to ask it in order to forestall simplified conclusions in our students. They are right to think that Walter Mitty is funny and weak, but there is evidence that the sympathies of the narrative voice in the story lie with Mitty, and the last sentence seems to indicate that that sympathy is not completely a product of pity; it has its note of admiration also. And this should lead us to a crucial question about the kinds of relevance which this story has. It does not simply condemn American society, or the American predatory female, out of hand. Neither is it asking us simply to condescend to the hero. It is asking for a complicated response in which we must contemplate the vitality of his imagination and extend some of our awe to its survival in the midst of loud and vulgar and endless threat. So that if "The Secret Life of Walter Mitty" is saying that the submerged American male is a comic figure in his only outlet against mistreatment and misunderstanding, it may also be saying that the mind has its own sources of valor.

Beginning, as I have tried to do, with a discussion of a specific work after very measured preliminary remarks about what to expect in the short story has the virtue of getting the student away from generalities quickly. It should, however, help to open another area of interest for definition and illustration. Let us hope that by the end of a first analysis our students have begun to get a sense of the kind of relevance a short story can have both in its focus on familiar experience and in its refusal to pigeonhole even its most stereotyped characters. Now is the time to point out that the refusal to pigeonhole—the refusal to give us back an uncomplicated image of ourselves—is often a more interesting aspect of the difference that a short story can make for us than its vividness of illusion. The way that the short story creates this kind of interest is through that peculiar quality of compression which we have seen patterning all the seemingly unrelated aspects of "The Secret Life of Walter Mitty" into a coherent whole.

But perhaps compression is not the precise word for this source of interest in the short story; we need a word that will remind us that out of the severe limitation in words, the short story characteristically gives us a sense of having participated in an experience which has grown enormously and is continuing to grow in our imaginations. A better word may be *economy,* for it is from the writer's saving use of every detail—of every image, of every nuance in speech or gesture, of the weight of every action and the significance of every object in the setting of his story—and it is from the craft with which he combines all these in his three thousand or more words that the short story attains its expansive quality. Typically, this economy stretches the reader's imagination to the past and the future which surround the story, and so we end by seeing the whole life of a Walter Mitty on the evidence of one carefully dramatized segment of it. Our view is not limited by the fullness of circumstance and analysis which is available to the novel reader. In the short story, all circumstance is revelatory, and most analysis requires an act of imagination on the reader's part.

But this economy in the short story is a planned economy; its suggestions are controlled, and although they demand the reader's cooperation, they do not permit him to cooperate at random. This controlled freedom, then, is the source of that interest in the short story which is essentially a matter of form and craft. We should broach it, once we have a good example within our experience, without apology; indeed I have found that by the time students have really thought about a complex, tightly constructed story, they are apt to become fascinated with the possible relations which they had missed at first reading, and they are awed by the writer's craft in having so subtly established those relations. I think that there is a great deal of latent and untapped interest among young people for the craft of fiction. I would suggest, for example, that the same interest which sends a young mechanic to the garage to tinker endlessly over the engine of his secondhand car may also inspire him to explore the interrelations among the elements which go to make up a short story.

Form and craft are difficult concepts to talk about, because the definitions for them rarely make much sense in the abstract, and to show what the abstractions refer to in specific stories requires an almost impossible hold on the story's many different elements— and all at the same time. Nevertheless, if we wish to find a legitimate way to solve the problem of getting our students to recognize not only the relevant connection between art and life but also the relevant difference, we must tackle this problem. We have seen that the short story gives us a genre which establishes the connection through its mode of familiar realism, but its economical use of that mode brings into play the great formal skill which emphasizes the fact that life is *arranged* consciously in art. Of course, poetry can provide this formal economy also, but I think that its special mode of metaphor, and the attendant verbal complexity, are usually added obstacles to the discussion of form as a natural and essential aspect of art with students. The short story's essential form unfolds through the internal logic of the story—both arising from and guiding the relations suggested by its subject. From this kind of form we can more easily pass to poetry and the relationship of conventional verse types like the sonnet to the kind of demand which his subject has posed for the poet and the kind of meaning which the conventional form makes available. There is, to be sure, a loose convention of length which will create some expectations of what a short story can do and what it cannot; but in order to perceive the organic forming principle of any single story, one must first be lost for a while as the patterns subtly begin to emerge through the insistences of certain images, or the repetitions of gesture, or the sudden emphases in action, or even the surprise of an ending.

In our discussions of the short story, then, we should try to show how the patterns begin to take shape by holding the whole work before the students while we shift back and forth with them to see what has caused that fine reverberation that comes with the last sentence. This kind of discussion is available only when the work has been read twice; and this is true for novels also. In all the novels I can think of, the sense of form must come with a second reading. *Pride and Prejudice, Great Expectations, Moby Dick,* and *The Great Gatsby* absolutely require a rereading or at least a rescanning if they are to assume their fullest artistic dimensions in the mind of the reader. And here is the problem of the novel for the high school teacher. He must do his best with a single reading of the novel, and as George Levine has suggested elsewhere in this book, give up for the moment the problem of form.

In summary, then, we have an advantage in teaching the short story because it has no strict conventions and it is short enough to be talked about in terms of its organic, natural, formal principles. Its special economy also assures us that every nuance and every detail has been calculated to establish that central pattern of meaning which will expand the limited subject in our imaginations. William Faulkner has put the case well in an interview with students at the University of Virginia: "In a short story that's next to the poem, almost every word has got to be almost exactly right. In the novel you can be careless but in the short story you can't. . . . You have less room to be slovenly and careless. There's less room in it for trash. In poetry, of course, there's no room at all for trash. It's got to be absolutely impeccable, absolutely perfect."

At this point in the discussion of form, I would like to shift back to the kind of verisimilitude which the short story offers. I want to return to that suggestive definition of the source of this formal quality of the genre as its interest in human loneliness. It is important for the student to see the functionality of form—its rootedness in the writer's vision of experience. If the writer is drawn again and again to the image of man locked within himself, spurned by misunderstanding and scorn into a life lived incommunicado, then the situations, entanglements, crises, and resolutions will be private; they will be acted out on a stage upon which the backdrop, the props, and the supporting actors, such as they are, make their prime signification through relationships with one another as well as through appeals to the commonly received assumptions about the nature of life. The writer has to form his vision in such a way that it will permit an intimate dramatization of the strange conflicts of the central character without relying on the "trash" of irrelevant detail or intrusive analysis.

G. K. Chesterton, in a study of Charles Dickens, defines incisively this kind of relationship between subject and form in the modern short story. "Our modern attraction to short stories is not an accident of form; it is the sign of a real sense of fleetingness and fragility; it means that existence is only an impression, and, perhaps, only an illusion."

It is important to establish a flexible concept of form in the short story at the very beginning of our treatment of the genre because such a foundation will determine the way in which we can approach the other aspects of narration. The elements of narrative are too well known to bear a great deal of discussion; I am sure that all teachers have some general ideas about plot, character, scene, setting, atmosphere, and tone. Moreover, the notes and introductions in most textbooks will provide a relatively common set of definitions and general rules of thumb. To avoid repetition of what is already available, I would like to choose only three elements of narrative which seem to me to need some rethinking. The three I have in mind are plot, symbol, and style. I believe that these frequently become crucial for the understanding of the short story and that they may be either oversimplified or neglected in discussion. Finally, it seems to me that a flexible handling of them in the classroom can answer a few more of the questions about literature which trouble our students.

I would suppose that every teacher has at one time or another run into the problem of the student papers which offer nothing but plot summary in their attempts to analyze a story. They come from students who think of a story as a sequence of actions only. They may have heard plot discussed in class; they may even have memorized a diagram which showed the usual sequence of action in a story—rising action, climax, and falling action. But the diagram probably confused them if they have failed to understand that plot concerns mainly the *causes* for actions. Even when the important element of causality in plot has been grasped, however, students may think that causality always takes the form of the motivations which impel the characters to act. If their papers summarize what the characters have done, and why, they will seem to have analyzed the story in the one way that makes sense.

The first step in rethinking this problem with our students must lie in denying them the pleasure of schematic clarity. We might point out that the diagram is more useful for the study of drama, where the nature of the form itself brings the issue of plot into sharper focus. In most plays, action and motivation are the major vehicles for meaning. Dialogue reveals the causes of the action, locating our interest squarely in the motives and behavior of the characters, and the resolution comes about through something significantly *done* on the stage. But prose fiction, which not only provides dialogue and action, but also sets the scene, establishes the atmosphere, and dramatizes the inner lives of its characters, can trace the causes of action to sources more varied than those to be found in what the characters say and do. There is a narrator, and the story he tells may perfectly well turn upon causes outside the characters—on blind fate, or a vagrant mood, or nothing more than his own sense of what some essentially undramatic situation means. In some short stories, there seems to be no plot at all, until the reader suddenly becomes aware that while he was not looking the narrator's attitude shifted slightly. In Conrad Aiken's "Silent Snow, Secret Snow," a major source of meaning in what would otherwise be a case history of insanity is the failure of the narrative voice to comment in any way on what is happening. The shift, the climax, lies in the reader's own increasing consciousness of something never registered openly in the account before him. Many modern short stories carry with them a delayed reaction, because "nothing happens"—until we think back over the lack of action and realize the importance of there having been none. James Joyce is among the finest masters of this curious technique, and he is also (the fact is no coincidence) one of the most influential short story writers of this century.

It is obviously unwise to start discussion of plot with an un- plotted story, but once the complexity of the problem has been established, I would suggest attempting a difficult and subtle ex- ample. The one I would like to treat here, "The Doll's House" by Katherine Mansfield, has a relatively simple and definite plot. Now, it is crucial to make quite clear when we begin talking about any particular element in a story that we are choosing only one focus among many. Students may become confused when they think that our approach is the only one possible, and that if they have not thought about a work in the way we have in class, they have missed the point completely. I would begin an explication of plot in "The Doll's House," then, by saying that there are many interesting things in the story. The characterization of the children, for example, is very subtle, and the way Katherine Mansfield makes the doll's house itself become almost a symbol of the Burnell family and its relation to the rest of the society of the little town in which it lives is intriguing. But we want to see here how she sets up the relationship between what happens and the reasons it happens in her story.

The first thing to note is the kind of action that occurs in "The Doll's House." At first glance it may seem to be a very bland story; nothing spectacular takes place in it. A friend has sent a gift to the Burnell children. It is a well-equipped and clever doll's house, and it causes quite a stir among the children. Then we see that it is going to enable them to be very popular at school, for it will be a privilege for the other children to be allowed to see the house. The first part of the story, then, is an exposition of the situation. But at school the first day, we begin to see two sources of complication. For one, we see that the sisters are not at all alike; the eldest is a self-centered little girl who will try to boss the whole show, while the youngest, Kezia, who seems to love the house for its own sake, will feel impatient about her sister. Secondly, and more importantly for the plot itself, we learn that there are two school children who will not be allowed to see the house. The reason for this rejection is clearly their social position. By the time all this has been set up, and we know that most of the children have seen the house, a strange thing happens in the story. The action changes in kind and in pace. Instead of generalized descriptions, we are offered a tightly constructed scene. One day at play time, the other children begin to taunt the little Kelveys for their poverty. A second scene follows, that very afternoon. Kezia is in the courtyard alone, and she sees the Kelveys coming down the road. On the spur of the moment, she lets them into the yard to see the wonderful house. But just as they are beginning to look closely at it, Aunt Beryl, one of the older Burnells, sees them and shoos them off. The story ends very quickly. We see the poor little girls sitting together, and realize that seeing the house has meant a great deal to them.

One of the merits of summarizing in this fashion is that we have

to leave a good deal out. It is often useful to summarize to make
sure that a class has gotten the basic outlines of a story straight,
but in doing so we need to point to the difference made by what
we have had to exclude. This is especially revealing in "The Doll's
House" because what happens is mixed so intimately with the
nature and situation of the characters that a plot summary must
also analyze the characters. We might ask at this point what the
action *does* to the characters in the story. In answering this question, students may be brought to see that the characters in this
story do not change; the action is not designed to show any of
them suddenly overcoming a temptation or reaching a new insight about themselves. At the end of the story, as far as we can
tell, all the characters are the same. Kezia has done something
daring and unusual in admitting the little girls into the courtyard,
but we do not see her after that act, and therefore we cannot tell
if the act has made a permanent impression on her. Aunt Beryl's
action is very dramatic, but we realize that it reinforces what she
already is. There is a shift at the end of the story to permit us to
see the Kelveys from the inside, but they are essentially the same
also; what has happened to them will not cause them suddenly
to realize the full extent of the injustice of their state—they are
accepting that state one more time when the story draws to a
close.

We might ask here, then, where the climax of the story lies, and
what makes it climactic. I think we can show that the climax resides in the sudden revelation which the *reader* gets—a revelation
which seems unavailable to the characters in the story. And the
main source of this reaction in the reader is not a character or even
any particular action; the source is the narrator herself, who has
been setting up the episodes in such a way that their meaning is
available only to the outside observer who has been given the key
for putting them all together and interpreting them.

There are many stories in which the action does not work in the
way it works in "The Doll's House." Katherine Mansfield's "The

Garden Party," for example, has a heroine much like the Kezia of "The Doll's House," and its subject is similar; nevertheless, its focus is quite different in that the actions converge on the Kezia character, forcing her to see the real cruelty in her treatment of the "lower classes." In this story the center of interest *is* the radical change of a character's perceptions, but in "The Doll's House" the interest lies in the reader's perceiving the nature of the snobbery which causes such unexamined cruelty. Kezia's reaction is crucial because she is the only member of the Burnell family who has any kind of compassion for the Kelveys. Aunt Beryl's reaction is also important, for although we see her only briefly in the exposition of the story, she becomes a major actor in the last scene, and we learn there in a very brief glimpse into her motives that she is nasty because she had become involved with a lower-class lover and has been threatened by him: "But now that she had frightened those little rats of Kelveys and given Kezia a good scolding, her heart felt lighter. That ghastly pressure was gone. She went back to the house humming." Finally, Our Else, the pathetic youngest and most silent of the Kelveys, provides us with a key reaction. She has the last word to say, "I seen the little lamp," and in saying that she gives us our recognition that the silence of the little girls has not come from stupidity or insensitivity. This revelation at the very end of the story takes our minds back to all that has happened in the story in order to resee it in terms of the weight which the Kelveys' awareness adds to it.

By now we can point out to a class why a paper on the story which simply tells what has happened, and simply concludes that "The Doll's House" is about two little girls who are mistreated by a family of snobs, is inadequate. For the interest of the story lies in the pattern of relations which it lays open for us in selecting various characters at crucial but unwary moments of everyday stress. I do not want to imply that in all "true" plots the characters have to be aware of the implications of what they have done by the end of the story; what I do want to reinforce here is the fact that in many short stories, the major source of the pattern is the spectator, guided by the selection of the narrative voice. Actions in short fiction may characteristically achieve their meaning from their relations with other aspects of the narrative rather than from the internal logic of their progression and what that progression reveals about the growth or decay of a central character. Perhaps this is what Frank O'Connor means when he says in *The Lonely Voice* that the short story has no hero. In most stories, "There is no character . . . with whom the reader can identify himself, unless it is that nameless horrified figure who represents the author."

The traditional plot is not, then, always the central aspect of the short story. Rather, we must look in the short story for relationships—for the way characters and episodes and setting and even the tone of voice of the author work together. There is an unusual use of tone in "The Doll's House" which might be worth pointing out to students to illustrate one of the more subtle ways action can be integrated in so short a space. Katherine Mansfield constantly shifts the focus through which events are seen in "The Doll's House." When the story begins, we first see the arrival of the doll's house through the eyes of the older Burnells; the narrator makes this clear by telling about it in their idiom, actually mimicking their voices.

> When dear old Mrs. Hay went back to town after staying with the Burnells she sent the children a doll's house. . . . And perhaps the smell of paint would have gone off by the time it had to be taken in. For, really, the smell of paint coming from that doll's house ("Sweet of old Mrs. Hay, of course; most sweet and generous!") —but the smell of paint was quite enough to make any one seriously ill, in Aunt Beryl's opinion.

Already we have been given evidence of the selfishness and neurosis of Aunt Beryl which will take its toll on the Kelveys and Kezia later. And immediately, when the house is described more fully, we are out of the idiom of the adults; we see the house through the eyes of the children, especially of Kezia: "But perfect,

perfect little house! Who could possibly mind the smell? It was part of the joy, part of the newness." In the remainder of the story, the tone which the adults take with the children and about them alternates continually with the tone of the children themselves, and this alternation helps us to begin to see the corruption of the Burnell children, who, in the scene in the play yard when they are taunting the Kelveys, take on the very gestures which they have seen their parents use. "Emmie swallowed in a very meaning way and nodded to Isabel as she'd seen her mother do on those occasions."

Another set of relations has been established by using the beautiful little lamp in the story as a test for the characters. The fact that Kezia loves the lamp—"But the lamp was perfect. It seemed to smile at Kezia, to say, 'I live here.' The lamp was real"—indicates her sensitivity. Isabel always forgets the lamp when she tells the other children about the house; she seems not to know what is real. But at the very end of the story we see that there is one other character who knows what is real. Our Else's one comment on the house establishes her relation with Kezia, " 'I seen the little lamp,' she said, softly."

I am not sure how much of the complexity of a short story like "The Doll's House" can be indicated in an hour's discussion; but it seems to me that the point to be made in such a discussion is that the problem of plot is going to lead inevitably to the other aspects of the short story which must come to bear so heavily on the eventual patterning of meaning which is characteristic of the genre. This interworking of all the aspects of narrative makes the short story an especially helpful form to use in the elucidation of the nature of plot in any narrative, for ordinarily plot is less simply extricable from the other elements of the short story than of any other literary form.

I have noted the presence of a possible symbolic weight in "The Doll's House" for the doll's house itself and for the little lamp which means so much to Kezia and to Our Else. Students may become fascinated with the revelations which an attention to the symbolic weight of a story can make, and they can go overboard. On the other hand, if we are not very careful about our approach to the problem, some students may become extremely disturbed by their own failure to understand or to "catch" the symbolic possibilities of a story. I have found this latter group of students far more prevalent, and I would like to begin this exploration of symbolism by attempting to suggest the impression they can get from some kinds of symbolic criticism.

To be able to assign abstract concepts to the elements in a story is a necessity for some temperaments which feel apologetic for the vagueness of the literary enterprise and which may even have given up the endeavor to make its "vagueness" seem relevant. A second possible source for confusion about symbolism—one that constitutes an almost hypnotic temptation—is less admirable. It resides in an unconscious effort to shock and amaze the uninitiated; to say to the unwary, "You who think you know everything, wait till you see what this *really* means!" And then from the farthest reaches of possibility the critic may pull a symbolic significance. He may practice a little amateur psychoanalysis; he may reveal a world shot through with difficulties, and penetrable by only the most acute, the most trained, the most subtle mind. Literature becomes a matter for the expert who can see deeply into the meanings which stories are always hiding rather than revealing; the teacher and critic becomes a kind of high priest, presiding over great mysteries, and the student may become overawed, ready to memorize where he does not understand the literary equations which have been set up.

Who has not succumbed to this temptation, especially when he has found a work really opening for him at the touch of a suggestion about its symbolic weight? Once we look at the Mississippi River as a "great brown god," then of course Huck Finn is going to become the American Adam and Mark Twain's novel will begin to take on the dimensions of a culture myth and we can talk about culture myths for the rest of the hour. But what will we miss in the meantime? We will miss the fact that Huck Finn is also to be seen as a real boy, more typical than symbolical (if I can make what seems to me to be a crucial distinction for a kind of signification which one finds in realistic literature), whose moral growth in his discovery of his brotherhood with the Negro Jim must be shared by a reader who has *not* been able to come to think of himself or the hero as "modern man" but as private, particularly fallible human beings whose change must come in the toil and sweat of a daily life rather than in abstraction.

The problem in an overenthusiastic approach to symbolism in a story may involve an oversimplification of literature, and it also may invoke a mysterious fog which would enable the student to make everything mean something else, and therefore in the end, I think, mean nothing immediately relevant at all.

I do not want to say that there is no such thing as symbolic fiction; I would suggest instead that we take great care to show our students how we must proceed to talk about symbolism. "The Lottery," a very popular story among students, might provide a good place to start. I would begin by asking what the difficulties of this story are. How do we know that it is not an ordinary, realistic story? What is left out? And what is continually insisting upon itself that has not been present in the other stories which have been read?

It is a good idea to take advantage of the obvious in our teaching, and certainly in getting to the symbolism in "The Lottery" I would start with the most obvious aspect of the story, the shock which explodes at the end. I think that we can be sure that every student will have registered this shock, and we should try to get him to see why that reaction was prepared for him and what it means in terms of the entire story. First of all, where does it come from? If we direct the student to the opening lines of the story, we can show that it comes in part from a contrast which has been carefully set up. "The morning of June 27th was clear and sunny, with the fresh warmth of a full-summer day; the flowers were blossoming profusely, and the grass was richly green." Such a setting gives no clue that the story which takes place in it will be a story of mob murder. And then as the story proceeds, it seems clear that the writer is not aiming to go very deeply into the inner nature of the inhabitants of the town. All of them seem typical; there are even some humorous details about the typical American families which are gathered there together. Mr. Martin has to look sharply at his wayward son; Mr. Summers is described with a little bit of gossipy insight. Even the names of the inhabitants of the town seem designed for their typicality; we could not point to any one of them as unusual. The setting and the characters, in fact, seem set up to give us a sketch of life in a small American town.

And that, indeed, is where the shock of the story begins to assume meaning. For if we do have a typical town with typical people in it, then the story is also saying that such a town and such people can typically condone the irrational destruction which closes the story. They can even insist on it at the risk of their own lives. Perhaps they even *have* to indulge in it.

Now we are ready to face the problem of what the story symbolizes. And here I would emphasize the fact that this story is *asking* us to make such an interpretation by refusing to give us the kinds of information which would make any other interpretation possible. Another dimension of the shock which we feel at the end of the story comes from the impossibility of clearly knowing what is happening or why. When we look back over the story, we can see that some explanations have been given. We can see that this village is described as any village, or every village, might be. So that already we are beginning to think of what happens in it as being typical. Moreover, we know that the lottery is a matter of tradition, and that everyone willingly participates in it, even though there is an indication that in some other villages it has been done away with. Abstracting the essential elements of the story, then, we can say that it is about the capacity of ordinary, likeable people to commit murder, brutal murder, because of a tradition which they blindly accept. And since the story will take us no farther, it seems logical to conclude that we are being invited to associate the story with any specific examples of such abstractions. We can go back as far as primitive human sacrifice, and we can go—really we are *asked* to go by the modern setting of the story—to our own time, where we may begin to think of the concentration camps, of political persecution, or even of small-town gossip as irrational games of chance which victimize even those who participate in them. It is an interesting aspect of "The Lottery" that Mrs. Hutchinson has been quite willing to play the game up to the time of her realization that she is its victim.

On this last detail, I would like to emphasize an aspect of symbolism which I think is crucial. Even in a story as frankly allegorical as "The Lottery" our interpretation is controlled to a large degree by the possibilities which the story excludes. I think, for example, that this story excludes any reading which makes Mrs. Hutchinson a traditional martyr figure. It refuses to do this, and in the process refuses to become an easy sermon on our favorite view of injustice, which places the responsibility on "the others" by emphasizing the fact that all the victims participate, and that there is no murmur of protest, even from the family of Mrs. Hutchinson. There is another problem closely attached to this one in this story. How are we to interpret any of the other actors in the lottery? I can imagine that some adventurous student, having been awakened to all the possibilities which the story holds, might want to make a religious allegory here. The village is the garden of Eden, he might say. Mr. Summers is God, Who metes out punishment. Tessie Hutchinson is Eve and her husband is Adam. The black box from which the lots are drawn stands somehow for the devil. I won't go on; the possibilities of this approach are too evident already. How can such an interpretation be handled? I would not sneer at it out of hand; I would simply ask, does it fit, or what part of it fits? It would soon become clear, for example, that if Mr. Summers is God, then he is a strangely inconsistent symbol. For he, too, is mortal, has to draw a lot, and is ignorant of the reasons for doing what he does. One problem in symbolic interpretation, then, is to determine what the context of the story excludes as well as includes. One of the things which "The Lottery" excludes is an oversystematization of its symbolism, and it excludes this by failing to give us any clear references to any system of myth.

Now I would like to make a distinction between formal symbolism that gives the images in the story clear reference to an abstract set of meanings and the kind of object which, as it becomes more and more important to a story, also comes to have extraordinary resonance. The little lamp in "The Doll's House" is an example of this. At first it seems unobtrusive; then it comes to signify the whole mystery and charm of the house for Kezia, and finally we see that it has had the same kind of appeal for little Else. By this time, it has symbolic weight in the story, but shall we go on to say that the fact that lamps give forth light makes this lamp stand for Truth? To insist upon a definite abstraction would do violence to the essential mode of Katherine Mansfield's story; nevertheless, some possibility seems to be there. I would emphasize the word "some," for it carries that sense of this object working mysteriously as a resonance rather than an equation. As Eudora Welty has said in "The Reading and Writing of Short Stories," "Every good story has mystery—not the puzzle kind, but the mystery of allurement. As we understand the story better, it is likely that the mystery does not necessarily decrease; rather it simply grows more beautiful." It is a mistake to think of symbolism as a puzzle which can be at last solved and put away, and that is why so puzzling a story as "The Lottery" is extremely valuable to us in teaching symbolism, for even though we can begin to unlock its meaning, we will find that its exclusions and qualifications will still resist and challenge and stretch our understanding.

The three stories I have mentioned so far have been relatively modern stories which use great simplicity of language and terseness of exposition to make their points. I am aware that I may be loading the scale too heavily on the side of one kind of short story. How shall we teach the older short story, the one which our students may find tiring and verbose? I will admit that this is a problem; I have found it very difficult to get a college class interested in such a work as Willa Cather's "Paul's Case" because the style seemed stodgy and redundant to them and because the meaning of the story seemed over-apparent and therefore trivial. I would like very briefly, then, to talk about the problem of style in the short story; I would suggest that we must emphasize the expressive qualities of prose if we are to prepare our students for the earlier masters of the short story who did not consider extreme economy of words an absolute necessity in their art.

Joseph Conrad's "Lagoon" is longer than most of the stories included in high school texts. It is long because of Conrad's devotion to setting; there is an introduction of several pages in which the passage of a canoe up a river and into the lagoon where the main story unfolds is described with great detail. Then as the Malay Arsat tells about how he had abandoned a brother to die at the hands of pursuers in order to steal away the woman he loved, the narrative is interrupted by several more long passages which describe the setting of the lagoon which has become his place of refuge. These are the passages the ordinary student will skip. I would begin by admitting this, and I would ask what the story is about without the description. The answers would probably say that it is about the betrayal of a brother, which is shown to have been in vain, because the woman for whom Arsat has left his brother is now, as he tells the story, on the verge of death. The pathos which such a shortened version of "The Lagoon" retains may seem sufficiently interesting to the student to justify his skipping all that prose which is "just description."

But then I would turn to ask what, if anything, the description adds to the story. And I would take the first long passage to study this question.

> The white man rested his chin on his crossed arms and gazed at the wake of the boat. At the end of the straight avenue of forests cut by the intense glitter of the river, the sun appeared unclouded and dazzling, poised low over the water that shone smoothly like a bank of metal. The forests, somber and dull, stood motionless and silent of each side of the broad stream. At the foot of big, towering trees, trunkless nipa palms rose from the mud of the bank, in bunches of leaves enormous and heavy, that hung unstirring over the brown swirl of eddies. In the stillness of the air every tree, every leaf, every bough, every tendril of creeper and every petal of minute blossoms seemed to have been bewitched into an immobility perfect and final. Nothing moved on the river but the eight paddles that rode flashing regularly, dipped together with a single splash; while the steersman swept right and left with a periodic and sudden flourish of his blade describing a glinting semicircle above his head. The churned-up water frothed alongside with a confused murmur. And the white man's canoe, advancing upstream in the short-lived disturbance of its own making, seemed to enter the portals of a land from which the very memory of motion had forever departed.

There are two elements of the story which become apparent from this passage. First, the story is told to a nameless white man whom we see here on his way to visit Arsat. Second, the forest through which he passes is described with an extraordinary emphasis on immobility and deadness. The insistence on rendering a *sense* of the forest, as well as its presence, shows the passage may be creating a frame for the story which is to commence later. It is not only the story itself which is to be seen, but the way in which the white man sees it, as connected somehow with the nature of the setting in which it is told. And so when Arsat begins to recall his tale for the white man as they wait for dawn and the death of the woman, a description of the threatening setting returns, this time made more precise by the white man's sense of evil.

The ever-ready suspicion of evil, the gnawing suspicion that lurks in our hearts, flowed out into the stillness round him—into the stillness profound and dumb, and made it appear untrustworthy and infamous, like the placid and impenetrable mask of an unjustifiable violence. In that fleeting and powerful disturbance of his being the earth enfolded in the starlight peace became a shadowy country of inhuman strife, a battle-field of phantoms terrible and charming, august or ignoble, struggling ardently for the possession of our helpless hearts. An unquiet and mysterious country of inextinguishable desires and fears.

It should begin to become more clear that the description is not primarily designed to add circumstantial detail. The world in which the story is told has a bearing on the meaning of the story for the white man; it forms an ironic contrast in all its immobility with the human strife which goes on within it. And so the pathos of Arsat's story does not reside in the death of his woman so much as in the fact that that death takes place in a world which does not care—which is brutish and silent—but which may also be responsible for the very drives that move men to rash actions. The jungle and the lagoon itself speak of this through Conrad's description. And then at the end of the story, Arsat seems to have recognized the meaning of the setting himself, for as we see him at the very end, he "Stood lonely in the searching sunshine; and he looked beyond the great light of a cloudless day into the darkness of a world of illusions."

In his eloquent "Preface" to *The Nigger of the Narcissus*, Conrad said:

Fiction—if it at all aspires to be art—appeals to temperament. And in truth it must be, like painting, like music, like all art, the appeal of one temperament to all the other innumerable temperaments whose subtle and resistless power endows passing events with their true meaning, and creates the moral, the emotional atmosphere of the place and time.

I think that through a careful investigation of the prose style of a short story like "The Lagoon" we can alert our students to "the moral, the emotional atmosphere of the place and time." And we must point out to them the two aspects of prose which make this moral atmosphere analyzable; that is, the aspect of tone and that of style. Tone in "The Lagoon" is conveyed through the character of the white man who observes the landscape and listens to Arsat's story. He provides the place for the reader to stand in the story, and it is through his reactions to the story and the jungle that the reader begins to see that the context of Arsat's tale is a sense of the universal possibility of darkness in the actions of a man. Moreover, the style reinforces this sense with its emphasis on adjectives of immobility, stillness, darkness, and despair. The very length of the sentences conveys the struggle and uncertainty involved in defining universality of the situation in which the white man finds Arsat. He is contemplating a darkness in the heart of the man which is as eternal and mysterious as the hidden and stagnant lagoon in which it is revealed. I have space only to suggest what is going on in Conrad's style in this story. A class discussion of it would take a more patient analysis. But such an analysis can help to open up a story which students have turned down because they have not thought of style as capable of the interest which they find in such things as plot and symbolism in fiction.

The art of teaching seems to me a matter of questions and answers; the best teachers I have known have been the ones who could outguess me—tell me what questions I was asking. I have tried to do some wholesale "outguessing" here because I have found that my own teaching has been most successful when I have had a relatively "antagonistic" group of students to work with—and by "antagonistic" I mean students who were either "stumped" or convinced that they could not "get" English literature. I have also found that when I did not have such antagonism in a class, the only way that I could get the learning started was to "stump" them myself with the most difficult work I could find. Because it is compact, and in its compactness extremely complicated, because it

contains either implicitly or explicitly all the evidence that is necessary in understanding it, because it has attracted most of the truly
significant writers of the twentieth century and therefore numbers
among its examples works of undoubted power and grace, the
short story frequently provides the devices to stump students in a
salutary way. It permits the teacher of English to ask questions
which interest students so intensely that they will spend an hour
with him searching for the answers, and it permits *them* to ask at
the end of such a period where they can find other stories which
will stump them and worry them again.

4

On Teaching Poems

PHILIP APPLEMAN

Associate Professor of English,
Indiana University

In Shiraz, near the heart of the ancient Persian Empire, stands a great alabaster mausoleum, dominating a hillside garden rich with roses, colonnades, reflecting pools, and lovely trees, orange and cypress and pine. Whose tomb is it? One of the more magnificent shahs? A fabulously wealthy Oriental merchant? Not at all; it is the tomb of Hafiz, a lyric poet contemporaneous with Chaucer. His hypnotic verses sing constantly from loudspeakers in the garden. It is a place of pilgrimage.

We have nothing at all like it in the nations of the West. The English cache their poets in one corner of Westminster Abbey; the French collect theirs in the Panthéon. Dante, it is true, has his own tomb in Ravenna, but it is a puny thing compared to the Emperor Theodoric's, on the other side of town. Stratford-on-Avon is itself a monument, but less a monument to Shakespeare than to the tourist industry. And America: how many of our two hundred million countrymen even know where Walt Whitman is buried?

This preoccupation with tombs is not just an idle fancy. It is all very well to say that a poet's monument is in your heart; but where your treasure is, there will your heart be also, and common-sense Westerners no longer lay up for themselves treasures in verse; not since the Renaissance. Before that, before we developed our well-known "dissociation of sensibility," before we undertook to be specialists in personal functions, putting our ratiocination on a Monday-Friday schedule and saving our emotions for weekends: before all that, it was possible to say (as Sir Philip Sidney could say, standing in the twilight of the Whole Man) that it was the poet who built the "treasure-house of Science" and developed "the noblest scope to which ever any learning was directed." Now, however, we tend, habitually and unquestioningly, to keep our hard-boiled common sense (the Darwinian side of the mind, a "machine for grinding general laws out of large collections of facts") at arm's length from our sensibilities (the Wordsworthian side of the mind, searching for "the primary laws of our nature" in "the spontaneous overflow of powerful feelings").

There is little point to arguing with history; nobody wants to go back to the manor house and the astrologers. Poets and teachers of poetry are stuck with the twentieth century, Two Cultures and all. What, then, can be done, short of exorcising the *Zeitgeist*, to enhance the estate of poetry? Some people are convinced that the public indifference to poetry today is the fault of the poets themselves—that their intentional "difficulty" and "obscurity" prove that they don't really care about the great unwashed public. Certainly one can hardly blame the average high school student for not being inspirited and rejoiced by Eliot's

> Here is the man with three staves, and here the Wheel,
> And here is the one-eyed merchant, and this card,
> Which is blank, is something he carries on his back . . .[1]

or Pound's

> Lie quiet Divus. I mean that is Andreas Divus,
> In officina Wecheli, 1538, out of Homer[2]

or Thomas'

> Abaddon in the hangnail cracked from Adam,
> And, from his fork, a dog among the fairies,
> The atlas-eaters with a jaw for news,
> Bit out the mandrake. . . .[3]

But the difficulty of modern poetry has been, I think, too much complained of. For one thing, all of the above poets had remarkable lyric gifts, and they have given us some of our most memorable (and not very difficult) poems: Eliot's "The Love Song of J. Alfred Prufrock," for instance, Pound's "The River-Merchant's Wife," Thomas' "Poem in October":

> It was my thirtieth year to heaven
> Woke to my hearing from harbour and neighbour wood
> And the mussel pooled and the heron
>   Priested shore
>   The morning beckon
> With water praying and call of seagull and rook
> And the knock of sailing boats on the net webbed wall
>   Myself to set foot
>   That second
> In the still sleeping town and set forth.[4]

For another thing, over the past ten or fifteen years, many of our poets (though not all of them), both in England and in America, have become more and more straightforward and less self-consciously learned than they had previously been for some decades. Howard Nemerov recently wrote, for instance:

Along with many others I learned from William Empson to value ambiguity; it was part of our purposeful labor, in those days, to fill our poems with somewhat studied puns which could be said to "work on several different levels" . . . I now regard simplicity and the appearance of ease in the measure as primary values, and the detachment of a single thought from its ambiguous surroundings as a worthier object than the deliberate cultivation of ambiguity.[5]

Much of our contemporary poetry has therefore become more available, more assimilable, to a wide public; axiomatically, this is a happy event for teachers of poetry. And there is a corollary: we have been blessed, at the same time, with a large number of very good and very productive young poets.

.   .   .

Teachers will probably agree that improving the estate of poetry depends partly upon better teaching; that is the subject of this essay. However, there are some serious obstacles to improving teaching in the high schools and junior high schools, and these should be acknowledged at the outset. For one thing, many high school English teachers are terribly overworked, meeting five large classes a day, as well as tending to all the humiliating household chores the school system traditionally foists upon them. Until their work loads are reduced, it is all but quixotic to expect consistently good teaching from the public school teachers. Part of every essay on the improvement of teaching ought therefore to be a stricture on wages and hours, addressed primarily to school administrators and school boards.

Admitting the difficult nature of the task, one may nevertheless discuss it; but there are other preliminary obstacles to good teaching, too. Some of our worst enemies, we should admit, lie within. "One of my first discoveries," F. Scott Fitzgerald wrote about college, "was that some of the professors who were teaching poetry really hated it and didn't know what it was about." One must hope that this affliction is not widespread among either professors or high school teachers; yet experience whispers, to anyone brave enough to listen to small voices, that the disease has spread further than we could like. It is hardly a curable disease; one cannot expect teachers of poetry who really and thoroughly dislike poems to wake up one bright morning suddenly admiring "Byzantium" or "The Emperor of Ice Cream." Nor can one realistically hope that all such teachers will spontaneously eye themselves with a fierce honesty and troop into principals' offices all across the republic, resigning their positions on grounds of incompetence. Short of such miracles, there is perhaps some hope in re-education—hope that a summer or two spent studying with professors who do like poetry, and who know how to communicate their liking, will work the needed cure. Fitzgerald's comment notwithstanding, such professors do exist.

Assuming, however, that a teacher of poetry knows his subject, likes it, and tries to convey his enthusiasm to his students, there are still all sorts of obstacles to doing the job well. For one thing, there is often, on the part of the students themselves, an outright hostility to school in general, to literature in particular, and to poetry very specially. I needn't analyze all the reasons for this hostility; anyone who has ever taught knows about it. What it portends is that we have to try very hard to "motivate" our students while avoiding the more obvious pedagogical blunders. It is not easy to sell a bumptious, gum-chewing, football-loving kid on poetry in the best of circumstances; if one starts on the wrong foot, it is almost impossible.

I want to propose, at the outset, that a poem may be a "good" poem and yet not a good "teaching" poem. Poetry lovers of long standing may forget or underestimate the force of this observation; we are so used to what is special about poetic language that we tend to accept it all without question, forgetting what a shock it may be to the beginner. Poetry *can* be shown to be close to the student's everyday experience, and of course it should be; but teachers have to work very carefully to manage it. One mistake that some teachers make (and many traditional high school textbooks as well, I'm sorry to observe) is to treat poetry as a historical phenomenon, starting the semester with "The Seafarer," laboring through "Sir Patrick Spens," selections from *The Canterbury Tales*, bits of *The Faerie Queene*, Shakespeare's sonnets, etc., and on to a climax with John Masefield or perhaps Stephen Spender. This is all well enough, I suppose, as history, but it is too often the death of poetry. By the time the students reach something that most of them might read with spontaneous and genuine pleasure, it is too late: they have had their turn with the thane of Hrothgar, the Red Cross Knight, cavalier thous and wilts and prithees, Scottish birkies and coofs, and so on; and their original hostility has been stoutly reinforced. A high school course in English should serve primarily the spirit of literature, not the fact of history. The most important thing for teachers to remember about the history of poetry is that it should always be presented backwards.

Another false start in poetry, I think, is the use of the long poem. To discuss a poem properly in the classroom, the teacher and students need to examine it closely, line by line. To do this with a long poem would take weeks, and most high school students' attention spans won't tolerate this. A sonnet is of course brief enough for intensive classroom work; so are the ballads in the "Basic Poetry Sequence for Grades Seven through Nine" in this series of volumes. *Il Penseroso,* however (a traditional favorite), seems to me to be at the outer limits of possibility. Longer poems might usefully be the subjects of outside papers or reports, once students have acquired experience in reading poetry, but are likely to be self-defeating as objects of class explication.

Still another false start, as far as most students are concerned, is the uncritically emotional approach. Much of the damage to the estate of poetry has been done, I believe, by people who consider themselves friends of poetry, who go dreamy-eyed at the mention of the word "poetry," and who then immediately and reverently stop thinking and bare their nerves to feel deeply. Emotion is an important ingredient of poetry, of course, and it would be a mistake simply to squelch those poetry lovers whose response seems excessive (even though one suspects that they love poetry considerably less than landscapes, sunsets, small animals, and the Deity); poetry today needs all the adherents it can get. Nevertheless, I think that the all too common conception of poetry-as-gush is one of the most ruinous enemies of the estate of poetry, because, for one very important thing, it alienates a great many young people. They may be silly children themselves, subject to all sorts of nonsense, fads, and crazes, but there are few of them who could feel comfortable facing a classroom full of their peers at eight-thirty on Monday morning and reciting, with feeling: "I pant, I sink, I tremble, I expire!" or "I fall upon the thorns of life! I bleed!" There are fashions in the demonstration of passion, and these lines are no more in style today than the chest-clutching and eye-rolling of the silent movies. They are, in short (because style is very important to the young), embarrassing. Furthermore, I suspect that, insofar as these poems communicate at all, they lead to other kinds of sentimentality (that mortal enemy of sentiment). The autoflagellations of the less-disciplined Romantics drive us steadily toward the little toy dog, staunchly and dustily awaiting the touch of a little hand, the smile of a little face.

There is a vast difference between any old emotion and the disciplined emotions of art. The cliché of the impractical, gushy, slightly effeminate poet is false to the facts of history. Chaucer was not impractical, gushy, or effeminate; neither, apparently, was Shakespeare; neither were Sidney or Milton or Johnson or Browning or Eliot or Stevens, or (as I remember literary history) most other poets. Nevertheless, the cliché tends to stick, encouraged by the misty-eyed among the poetry lovers themselves. I do not want to promote a false-hair-on-the-chest school of poetry appreciation; but poetry has, after all, for the greater part of history, managed to exist independently of the excesses of uncritical romanticism. This, for instance, is a characteristic passage from *Beowulf*:

> mæg Hygelāces
> hæfde be honda; wæs gehwæþer ōðrum
> lifigende lað. Līcsār gebād
> atol æglæca; him on eaxle wearð
> syndolh sweotol, seonowe onsprungon,
> burston bānlocan.
>
> (Hygelac's brave nephew had him by the hand—
> then each, alive, was hateful to the other. The horrid
> monster met with body-hurt; a wound showed wide
> and clear along his shoulder; sinews sprang apart,
> bone-locking muscles burst.[6])

That is powerful poetry, some of the earliest we have in English, and it is not a bit dreamy-eyed or teary. Neither is this, from Robert Frost:

When stiff and sore and scarred
I take away my hand
From leaning on it hard
In grass and sand,

The hurt is not enough:
I long for weight and strength
To feel the earth as rough
To all my length.[7]

That is deeply personal and deeply felt; but it is clear-eyed and in contemporary taste and therefore not embarrassing. And here are some lines of Wilfred Owen's:

Gas! Gas! Quick, boys!—An ecstacy of fumbling,
Fitting the clumsy helmets just in time,
But someone still was yelling out and stumbling
And flound'ring like a man in fire or lime.
Dim through the misty panes and thick green light,
As under a green sea, I saw him drowning.

In all my dreams before my helpless sight
He plunges at me, guttering, choking, drowning.[8]

That is good poetry, too, taut with emotion, but not silly emotion or selfish emotion or make-believe emotion. It is not a dainty poem or a foreign-sounding poem or a long poem or an old-fashioned poem. For all these reasons, it sounds as though it might have been written (as it was) by a sensible, recognizable, and gifted twentieth-century man who was honestly and powerfully moved to intense statement. It is therefore assimilable to young people in a way "I pant, I sink" is not.

All this may sound as though I am conducting a vendetta against the Romantic poets. No: my point is only that they are not the best poets to start out with. I believe that the way to approach the valuable work of the Romantics—and of most of the earlier poets, for that matter—is to begin by grounding students firmly in poets of their own time. Then, when it has been established that poetry is a valid kind of experience, one can lead the students to less familiar kinds of poetic language, including the more demanding poems of the Romantics themselves: to a poem like "Tintern Abbey," for instance, which, although firm with poetic hardness and specificity ("little lines of sportive wood run wild"), nevertheless moves on to a more abstract, less easily accessible kind of experience ("The still, sad music of humanity" and "We see into the life of things").

Once the students are past the beginning stage, it can be safely (if tactfully) revealed to them that a poem may well be a good poem even if they do not respond quickly or favorably to it. This may surprise some of them; the analogy of the television popularity ratings has no doubt misled some young people, as it has most of our advertisers, to believe that if a thing is worth doing at all, it is worth doing at the adolescent level. A better analogy to the criticism of poetry, however, and one that the student should easily understand, is Socrates' example of the expert horse-trainer, the man who *knows* better than others. Further examples can be drawn from nuclear physics or the building trades or surgery; in the arts, as in all these, there is no such thing as democratic rule. Only the expert counts. There is, on the other hand, tradition; and if literary tradition has it that Donne and Hopkins are good poets, then students should eventually come to see that, in simple fairness, they owe Donne and Hopkins an honest try, whether or not their poetry reads easily. Tradition, although not democratic, is not totalitarian, either. Most students will be intrigued, I believe, to learn the real meaning of "aristocracy," as distinguished from snob-rule. And they should approve of the justice of a continuing traditional judgment—constantly in process of revision, admitting mistakes about fashionable poets and recognizing the omissions of neglected ones —by generations and even centuries of the critical *aristoi*.

.   .   .

To some scholars, teachers, and poetry lovers, the foregoing will seem needlessly negativistic and unambitious; so perhaps I should repeat that I am trying to be thoroughly practical: what are we to do with the "average" student who comes to us bearing a dead weight of indifference or hostility to poetry? For the high school teacher of poetry, that is a grave and unavoidable question. One unfortunate part of the answer is that sometimes we shall simply fail. We may as well admit, to begin with, that some students will be untouchable by any approach possible in an ordinary class. That is not cynicism; if we fail to recognize the currently unavoidable limitations of our craft, we may either become too easily discouraged or pursue impossible tasks to the detriment of possible ones.

Another part of the answer—and a happier one—is that sometimes we shall succeed, and poetry will become a valuable part of some students' lives. Poetry, Auden said, makes nothing happen; but although poetry may never make Ireland sunny, or even sane, it may do many other things. One of its more earnest practitioners insisted that poetry is a criticism of life; it is not the vogue these days to insist upon it, but poetry does often make an appeal to the reader's character. That, incidentally, is partly why bad poetry is sometimes popular: it appeals baldly and seductively by means of stock emotional temptations. Good poetry also makes demands, but not cheap or easy ones: it reaches out to the reader's emotional discipline, to his humane sympathies, to his capacity for self-criticism, to the soundness of his faith or his doubt or his patriotism. Consider, for instance, the intricate play of sympathies in James Wright's remarkable sonnet, "Saint Judas":

> When I went out to kill myself, I caught
> A pack of hoodlums beating up a man.
> Running to spare his suffering, I forgot
> My name, my number, how my day began,
> How soldiers milled around the garden' stone
> And sang amusing songs; how all that day
> Their javelins measured crowds; how I alone
> Bargained the proper coins, and slipped away.

> Banished from heaven, I found this victim beaten,
> Stripped, kneed, and left to cry. Dropping my rope
> Aside, I ran, ignored the uniforms;
> Then I remembered bread my flesh had eaten,
> The kiss that ate my flesh. Flayed without hope,
> I held the man for nothing in my arms.

Or follow the uncompromisingly honest emotions of the last lines of Robinson Jeffers' "Hurt Hawks":

> I'd sooner, except the penalties, kill a man than a hawk;
>   but the great redtail
> Had nothing left but unable misery
> From the bone too shattered for mending, the wing that trailed
>   under his talons when he moved.
> We had fed him six weeks, I gave him freedom,
> He wandered over the foreland hill and returned in the evening,
>   asking for death,
> Not like a beggar, still eyed with the old
> Implacable arrogance. I gave him the lead gift in the twilight.
>   What fell was relaxed,
> Owl-downy, soft feminine feathers; but what
> Soared: the fierce rush: the night-herons by the flooded river
>   cried fear at its rising
> Before it was quite unsheathed from reality.

Or notice the wry, provocative reversals of conventional morality in John Crowe Ransom's "The Equilibrists":

> Full of her long white arms and milky skin
> He had a thousand times remembered sin.
>
> . . . .
>
> They burned with fierce love always to come near,
> But Honor beat them back and kept them clear.
> Ah! the strict lovers, they are ruined now!
> I cried in anger.

Or think of the challenge posed by Archibald MacLeish's "Land of the Free":

> We wonder whether the dream of American liberty
> Was two hundred years of pine and hardwood
> And three generations of the grass

And the generations are up . . .

We wonder whether the great American dream
Was the singing of locusts out of the grass to the west and the
West is behind us now:
The west wind's away from us:

We wonder if the liberty is done:
The dreaming is finished

We can't say

It is possible to read and enjoy all of these poems without agreeing
with the abstract ideas of their authors; but one has not read the
poems properly unless one has seriously pondered the complex
emotions, the sharp ironies, the moral challenges, of these lines.
In this way, without being consciously moralistic or didactic, good
poetry does have something to do with the reader's personal large-
ness, his maturity, his wisdom.

Still, this is not the first function of poetry. Poetry is not written
for purposes of mental health or general education or the social
weal. A poem is an experience which is an end in itself, not a means
to an end. Imagine someone alone somewhere, reading Gerard
Manley Hopkins' "Spring and Fall."

> Márgarét, are you griéving
> Over Goldengrove unleaving?
> Leáves, líke the things of man, you
> With your fresh thoughts care for, can you?
> Áh! ás the heart grows older
> It will come to such sights colder
> By and by, nor spare a sigh
> Though worlds of wanwood leafmeal lie;
> And yet you wíll weep and know why.
> Now no matter, child, the name:
> Sórrow's spríngs áre the same.
> Nor mouth had, no nor mind, expressed
> What heart heard of, ghost guessed:
> It ís the blight man was born for,
> It is Margaret you mourn for.

Assume that the reader has responded adequately to this poem—to its themes, to its ironies, to its tone, to its images, to its rhythms and its musical sounds: the experience then needs no further justification than that it has happened. It may not yet have occurred to some students (or to some adults), but this is precisely what life is all about. This experience is the reason, finally, for the alphabet, for language, for books, for schools. And it is much more. It is also the reason for computers, for the forty-hour week, for the combine, for the electric light; it is the reason for Salamis, Lepanto, Belleau Wood, and Okinawa. The full enjoyment of a fine work of art is an end product of civilization. It is one of a small number of human activities that is totally mature and totally self-justifying. Other activities may be necessary in order to go on living; this one is living itself. It is where we stop giving reasons.

GETTING STARTED

There are not many ways for a teacher to solicit outside help in the classroom, but there is one very easy way: selecting a good textbook. Some teachers prefer to teach poems without anyone else's editorial comment or "apparatus," for a number of reasons: because, for instance, the apparatus itself often needs explaining or criticizing (which diverts attention from the poetry), or because students tend to substitute a knowledge of the apparatus for the real experience of poems. On the other hand, a textbook that says more or less what the teacher wants to have said reinforces the student's learning: *repetitio mater est studiorum*. For this reason, time can be saved in class; the teacher can build on what the student has read. In any case, the method of making assignments is important. The act of assigning a chapter—or a group of poems—should be more than a simple reeling-off of page numbers. A teacher ought to explain briefly what the subject of the forthcoming assignment is, and ought further to read aloud (presumably the first of several oral readings) one or more of the shorter poems in the assignment. This will help the student not only to understand the subject but also to realize that studying a poem is a more complex act than simply glancing through it once. Incidentally, one may always assign more poems for study than one intends to discuss in class, but the number should never be so great that the students are tempted to skip through them rather than to read and reread them.

·   ·   ·

Another caveat: I believe it is a mistake to begin with abstract definitions. As far as I know, no one has ever defined "poetry" to anyone else's satisfaction; indeed, the sorry efforts of the best dictionary-makers suggest that no one has ever defined it to his own satisfaction. In any case, definitions and categorizing are almost always boring and almost never helpful to students. The student will find out what "poetry" is when he has experienced a number of poems.

I do not mean, of course, that the dictionary has no place in the study of poetry; on the contrary, since poets are more than usually resourceful with words, the student may have to become more familiar with his dictionary than he has ever been before. If he learns some new words, and gets used to learning new words, so much the better. It would be a pity, though, if he began to think of poems as mere word-puzzles; I would therefore suggest that the teacher always supply, along with the assignment, whatever information the students will need in reading a poem, beyond ordinary dictionary work. Why should the student be forced to find out, on his own, what "gestis" means, or "anneuche," or to resort to the encyclopedia to read up on the Waldensian sect or to find out what in the world a ball turret was, on some ancient craft called a Flying Fortress? The average high school student is and ought to be a layman, not a research scholar.

Essential "background" knowledge should be supplied by some system of footnotes, then, either written or oral, because poetic-reward should always outweigh fuss-and-bother by as wide a margin as possible. This is an important principle in making poetry available and enjoyable to students.

.　　　　.　　　　.

Some methods of getting started teaching poems are very simple but nevertheless effective. For instance, I think it is a good idea to begin with short poems that appeal to some special interest of the student's—like the classic example of the boy who enjoys "To an Athlete Dying Young" because he happens to be on the track team, or the girl who likes "To Autumn" because she happens to like autumn. It is true that these are only threshold interests, but they are one way to attract students to poetry. Another way is to use good light verse, like Frost's "Departmental," Carroll's "Jabberwocky," Reed Whittemore's "A Day with the Foreign Legion," or Anthony Hecht's "Samuel Sewall." There is some very bright play in these poems, and this should appeal to students. Narrative poems sometimes appeal quickly, too, because of the element of story, and lyrics because they are brief and intense. Teachers should test out the attractions of specific poems for themselves.

Another way of getting started with poems is to disarm any lurking suspicions that poetry is a totally alien kind of experience. In teaching the various elements of poetry, one can appeal to things the students are already familiar with. When talking about the sounds of poetry, for instance, one might mention that politicians, who depend totally on their appeal to all sorts of people, have always recognized the magic of certain combinations of sounds: "Win with Wilkie!" "I like Ike!" "All the Way with L.B.J.!" Advertisers, too—presumably practical men—recognize the attractiveness of such "poetic" devices as alliteration ("Surround it with Saran," "Reach for the Red Refresher," "Jolly Green Giant"); rhyme ("Look for the seal on the peel," "Hate that gray? Wash it away"); and onomatopoeia ("Snap, Crackle, Pop").

So, too, with that awesome subject, symbolism: it can be made to seem less formidable by asking, for instance, why our advertisers urge us to put tigers in our tanks. Such examples will date very quickly; the teacher should either keep them up to date or not use them at all. More timeless examples of symbolism abound, however: we might ask our students why they would be shocked if one of them were to trample on a piece of cloth bearing fifty stars and thirteen red and white stripes. And why is it that dimes and quarters made mostly of copper are worth as much as those made of silver, or why are paper dollars worth as much as silver ones? This is a beginning; inventive teachers can think up more and better examples. It is an essential part of the game, though, to show how a good poet uses all of these devices *better* than they are ordinarily used: more richly, more subtly, with more sensitivity to their possibilities, with more unity of effect.

TALKING ABOUT POEMS

In class discussions of poems, there is of course no mandatory starting place.*What may be an advisable beginning with one poem or with one group of students may not be advisable with another. Often, however, it makes sense to begin with meanings. I use "meanings" in the plural partly because I want to avoid endorsing the idea that a poem has *a* meaning; good poems are crowded with meanings. I have already mentioned that some of the problems of poetic meaning (lexicographical, biographical, historical) are in the

* Incidentally, teachers will recognize that this chapter is part of the larger series of essays on teaching poetry issued by the English Curriculum Study Center at Indiana University. The plan of that series, as concerns poetry, is to introduce sequential instruction in the junior and senior high schools. Emphasis in the seventh grade will be upon sound and story; in the eighth and ninth grades upon idea, picture, and metaphor; and, in grades ten through twelve, upon a deeper and richer experience of all of these things. Obviously what I have to say here will be somewhat more useful to teachers of the later grades, who can take more for granted in their approach to the subject; but teachers in junior high school, too, will—I hope—find suggestions that are relevant to their more circumscribed tasks.

nature of impedimenta and should be dealt with summarily. Beyond that, though, there are many kinds of meaning that will profit from class study. One such kind of meaning is the meaning of connotation. In "Desert Places," for instance, Robert Frost talks about "benighted snow." Everyone presumably knows the dictionary meanings of both of those words; but what more is Frost doing, one should ask, than merely giving an objective description? Other words in the poem need similar investigation: why the repetition in "night falling fast, oh fast"; and why does he use the word "scared," later on?

Allusions will often need explaining, too. What is the point of Cummings' title, "A Man Who Had Fallen among Thieves," or Frost's "Out, Out—"? Why does Eliot have Prufrock say he is not Prince Hamlet, and why are the women around Prufrock talking of Michelangelo? Why should MacLeish entitle a poem "You, Andrew Marvell" and why does he mention Ecbatan and Palmyra? The answers to these questions cannot always be "looked up" by inexperienced students. Nevertheless, they need answering if the poems are to have their full share of meaning.

It is important to the meanings of a poem, too, to recognize irony when it appears—not only verbal ironies approaching sarcasm, like Kenneth Fearing's description of contemporary man, "soothed by Walter Lippmann, and sustained by Haig and Haig" but the larger and more dramatic ironies of, say, the proud Ozymandias reduced to rubble, or Ransom's gentle but insistent irony over a dead lady "of beauty and high degree":

> Was she not lucky? In flowers and lace and mourning,
> In love and great honour we bade God rest her soul
> After six little spaces of chill, and six of burning.[9]

If it is true, then, as one poet put it, that

> A poem should not mean
> But be[10]

it is true in a very special way. A poem should not "mean" in the sense that the reader should satisfy himself with a prose paraphrase of it, or look for one line that seems to give the "message" of the whole poem. But it is only when the various kinds of "meaning" in a poem (including the meanings of metaphor, rhythm, and sounds) are all accounted for that the poem can properly "be," for the reader, at all. It is that kind of being which establishes its own justification, its own kind of truth; and without being doctrinaire or dogmatic, the teacher should aim a class toward that kind of meaning. In the process, it will sometimes be necessary to show that some meanings are better than others, that one person's opinion may not be as good as the next person's, and that it is a mistake to settle for simplistic or uninformed or inconsistent meanings in the work. A good poem may be complex—even ambiguous—but it has to be itself, its own, total self, not something else.

.　　　.　　　.

One kind of meaning in poems is the meaning of tone or attitude. Here the teacher will often encounter a hard problem of simple understanding: many students have difficulty distinguishing the poet's attitudes from his ideas. They no doubt *feel* some difference between:

> And all that mighty heart is lying still[11]

and

> "Well, Mr. Flood, if you insist, I might."[12]

But when asked to explain the difference in tone, they all too often say something like: "Wordsworth is talking about a sleeping city, and Robinson is talking about a drinking man." The teacher may find it a useful exercise to drill the students in the right *kind* of words to use in describing tone ("angry," "happy," "reverent," "sarcastic," "sad," "passionate," "supercilious") and to ask the students to stay strictly with such single words until the concept of tone is well learned; whereupon the better students may develop more extended and subtle explanations. In such exercises, poems having abrupt changes of tone are particularly useful, as, for instance, Drayton's shift from the false indifference of:

> Since there's no help, come let us kiss and part—
> Nay, I have done, you get no more of me

to the desperate sincerity of:

> Now at the last gasp of Love's latest breath . . .
> From death to life thou might'st him yet recover.[13]

.   .   .

Another way a poem means—or exists—is by appealing to our senses through imagery and metaphor. Not every poem works in the same way; some are richly sensuous, others comparatively bare; but it would be an odd poem indeed that made no claim on the senses at all. Students sometimes share the general misconception of poetry as something misty, vague, and generalized; they should be disabused of this notion by constant reference to the concreteness of poems being discussed:

> . . . Bare ruin'd choirs where late the sweet birds sang[14]
>
> . . . golden lamps in a green night[15]
>
> . . . A sunny Pleasure-dome with caves of ice[16]
>
> . . . in a wailful choir the small gnats mourn[17]
>
> . . . tired eyelids upon tired eyes[18]
>
> . . . quench its speed i' the slushy sand[19]
>
> . . . Why should I let the toad *work*
> Squat on my life?[20]

It is the *fact* of concreteness that matters, not its nomenclature; beyond simple sense-imagery lies the fascinating world of metaphor, and in that world are seductively technical words: metonymy, allegory, personification. It is all very well to ask students to memorize the definitions of some of these, but that act is less important than recognizing the meaning and value of the figures themselves. They are an important kind of meaning.

.　　.　　.

The same warning holds for the sound effects of poetry. It is always a strong temptation to pay too much attention to nomenclature: alliteration, onomatopoeia, consonance, cacophony. But the important thing in poetry is not that the student has come across these terms but that he hears and appreciates the music of:

> The packet's smooth approach, the slip,
> Slip of the silken river past the sides,
> The ringing of clear bells[21]

or:

> What passing bells for these who die as cattle?
> Only the monstrous anger of the guns.
> Only the stuttering rifles' rapid rattle
> Can patter out their hasty orisons.[22]

.　　.　　.

When Ben Jonson said of John Donne that he should have been hanged "for not keeping of accent," he was exhibiting a basic dilemma in the discussion of poetry: the rhythms of inferior poems (Boomlay, boomlay, boomlay, boom) may be open to public inspection; the rhythms of better poems may be so subtle or so original that even other poets will sometimes misunderstand them. Part of the problem, in our time, is, as George Levine mentions elsewhere in this volume, that "the language of poetry and the language of prose have become in many cases indistinguishable." Free verse *has* rhythm—that is what it means to be verse—but there is precious little point in applying traditional prosodic labels to:

> So much depends
> upon

> a red wheel
> barrow[23]

or:

> and break onetwothreefourfive pigeonsjustlikethat.[24]

But the problem is not an altogether new one, as Jonson's misunderstanding of Donne shows. Good poetry has never been mechanically regular in its rhythms. Sonnets, students are told, are written in iambic pentameter; but this line is certainly not iambic:

> When to the Sessions of sweet silent thought[25]

nor is this:

> I waked, she fled, and day brought back my night[26]

nor this:

> Plain living and high thinking are no more.[27]

The fact is that rhythm, the most important of all the elements of poetry, is the least discussable. This is partly because teaching rhythm is not like teaching imagery, which can be done, in part, by putting your finger on a word that represents something physical: a leaf, hair, glass. Teaching rhythm is like teaching the violin or handwriting or tennis: to teach it at all, the instructor has to depend upon a certain physical ability in the student. The degree of this ability varies from person to person, and is quite unpredictable. A student who is very good at spelling and imagery may be very bad at handwriting and rhythm. It is not always his fault; he simply may not *hear* rhythms. I have known a number of otherwise good students who were utterly incapable of describing the beat of "The curfew tolls the knell of parting day." This is a great pity, and it reminds us again that the hand of the Potter sometimes shakes. But there is very little, I am afraid, that the teacher of poetry can do about it; some of our students will never be great violinists and some will never fully enjoy the rhythms of poetry.

Fortunately, these aural cripples are a minority. What, then, should we do about the majority who are capable of putting the accent marks on the right syllables? (Some of them, incidentally, will be capable of hearing rhythms better than some of their teachers.) It ought to go without saying that the real work with rhythms should be oral work. One might begin with poems having obvious (that is, pronounced) rhythms—like a record of Richard Wilbur's reading of "Love Calls Us to the Things of This World"—and let the students quietly tap out the beat with one finger, on their desks. After a verse or two of this, one student may be asked to tap out the beat loudly, and the class might consider whether they agree with that student's feel of the beat. Certain aspects of Wilbur's rhythm will no doubt yield a consensus: that there are either four or five major stresses to most of the lines, for instance. There will be more argument over subtler matters of rhythm—over "secondary" beats, pauses, and so on—but even this disagreement can be used profitably in a poetry class.

In dealing with metrical poems, those students who can hear rhythms at all should soon be able to identify and describe the metrical patterns ("five beats to a line, and a ta-*tum* movement"). In doing so, they will also notice that even metrical lines are not always perfectly regular, and that the irregularities can sometimes be examined productively. When Shakespeare wrote this line, in sonnet 129:

> Savage, extreme, rude, cruel, not to trust

he broke the general metrical pattern of his poem; why? The students ought to speculate upon various possible reasons (variety, emphasis, regulation of tempo, incompetence) and try to decide which of them are applicable here. Is the poem better or worse for this metrical irregularity? The answers to these questions should reveal to the student something genuine about poets' use of rhythm.

There are other aspects of prosody that can be usefully studied in the classroom. One can compare lines like:

> So all day long the noise of battle roll'd
> Among the mountains by the winter sea[28]

with lines like:

> Sweet and low, sweet and low,
> 　Wind of the western sea[29]

or lines like:

> I watched out of the attic window
> The laced sway of family trees,
> Intricate genealogies[30]

and ask whether the rhythms seem appropriate to the poems, and why. Does the shortness (or longness) of some lines seem to fit or not to fit? How about the movement of ta-*tum* or *tum*-pa, or something else: does the rhythm seem too bumptious for the poem? Does it drag? Does it get monotonous?

·　　　·　　　·

I have not yet made any mention of the traditional prosodic terminology—iambic pentameter, trochaic tetrameter, etc.—because I want to encourage the idea that one can discuss the rhythms of poetry without a special vocabulary. Too often, I believe, teachers' emphasis on terminology has substituted for genuinely useful work with the actual rhythms of specific poems: students have learned to rattle off the big words facilely, *instead* of trying to hear what the rhythm of a poem is really doing; and harried teachers, glad to have something tangible and technical-sounding to cling to, have sometimes been willing parties to this fraud.

Each teacher will have to make up his own mind about the usefulness of the conventional prosodic labels. For my part, I almost always find the labels more bother than they are worth, and (except for iambic pentameter, which occurs so often that it seems

to me more awkward to avoid it than to use it) I assign them only
on an optional basis.

. . .

No matter how simple and nontechnical we make our discussion, though, some students will call it "picking the poems apart"
(not a bad definition, by the way, of the word "analysis"). They
mean, of course, that they don't like it and think it shouldn't be
done at all: they would apparently prefer simply to gasp in ecstasy
at poems they immediately like and shrug off those they dislike.
This sort of reacting may have some virtues, but they are not the
virtues that will, in the long run, help the estate of poetry. The
simple reactor-to-poetry is necessarily either a critical anarchist,
for whom discussion and communication are irrelevant or impossible, or a kind of incipient dictator, who believes that everyone
else ought to respond in the same way he does. In either case, his
attitude precludes the possibility of talking about the good and
bad qualities of particular poems.

Analysis of poems need not be pseudo-technical or mechanical.
Properly done, it is a very natural sort of movement from one aspect of a poem to another, a movement from rather simple uses
of the students' experience to more complex judgments of tone,
imagery, and so on. The movement should always eventually return to the starting point—the poem as a whole—and, it is to be
hoped, to the fullest possible experience of the poem. Then, de-
pending upon the skill of the teacher and the ability and sensitivity
of the students, the result ought to be a high ratio of reward to
effort and an enjoyment so rich that the student will be motivated
to read carefully the next poem he sees, and the next.

A poem should never be put aside until it is read well, aloud.
Ideally it should be read aloud at least three times: toward the
beginning of the study, at home by the student, and again in class
by a student volunteer or by the teacher or by a performer on
record. It should be emphasized to the class that this appeal-

through-the-ear is important; it should always be done as skillfully as possible.

Experience and a little ingenuity will suggest a number of ways to stimulate and hold students' interest in poems. This is, for instance, one of the fields in which audio-visual materials are especially useful. A student who has watched the puckish, spongy face of Robert Frost, as he says a poem and discusses it, will have reinforced that poem in the best possible way: by seeing and hearing an author whose voice and manner complement the poem perfectly. If for some reason it is impracticable to use one of the various movies that are available on Frost, there are many recordings of his readings which can very easily be worked into a class hour.

These days there are more and more poets available on records; in some instances, actors read well from deceased poets' work: James Mason does a brilliant job with Browning; Richard Burton reads Hardy; Paul Scofield does Dryden; Sir Ralph Richardson reads Blake, Coleridge, and Keats; and so on. Probably more interesting to students are the contemporary poets who have recorded their own work: Auden, Cummings, Eliot, Frost, MacLeish, Marianne Moore, Pound, Sandburg, Stevens, Thomas, Wilbur, Williams, Yeats, and others. These records are available at a discount to members of the National Council of Teachers of English; catalogues of the material can be had from the NCTE, 508 South Sixth Street, Champaign, Illinois, 61820. Several films on poetry can be obtained through the Audio-Visual Center, Indiana University, Bloomington, Indiana, and sometimes from the poets' publishers.

.   .   .

Implicit in the study of poetry is the assumption that some poems are better than others: richer, more cogent, more keenly observed, and ne'er-so-well-expressed. Therefore, another useful and standard exercise which the teacher might undertake (preferably after the class has had a rather substantial experience with poetry) is a close look at some bad poems. This can be a tricky project, because some students in every class will inevitably *like* the horrible examples, and the teacher may suddenly find himself with an argument on his hands. The student's defense of a bad poem will often be, "But if some people (or *I*) like it, doesn't that make it all right?"

Of course there is point to the question. The poems that most people turn to in their troubles, Auden once wrote, are "grotesquely bad verses written by maiden ladies in local newspapers." What one has to get students to understand (and it is not always easy) is the difference between personal or social usefulness, on the one hand, and literary value, on the other. The following are lines from an elegy I recently clipped from a small-town newspaper:

> In our hearts your memory lingers,
> Sweetly tender, fond and true.
> There's not a day, dear Elmer,
> That we do not think of you . . .

The personal usefulness of these lines may have been considerable. They no doubt gave the writer something to do for a time and they probably expressed the state of things in such a way as to comfort the writer, other members of the family, and, possibly, other bereaved townspeople who happened to read through the classified ads that day.

The distinction the teacher should try to make clear is that these responses depend upon the emotional condition of the writer and the presumed readers, rather than on the literary qualities of the verse itself. Study of a few bad poems should serve both to make this clear to the student and, at the same time, to make him a better judge of better poems.

Which of the many readily available bad poems should one use? "Trees" has been a favorite whipping boy at least since the

Brooks and Warren assaults on its confused imagery, its loose structure, its monotonous rhythm, the non-sense of its themes, and its appeal to stock responses. "Little Boy Blue" is also a perennial favorite bad poem; so are "Invictus," "If," and the entire canon of Edgar Guest—to cite only a few examples. An instructive exercise, I think, is to place side by side two poems having the same general set of themes, one a good poem and the other patently bad. One might compare Keats' "When I Have Fears That I May Cease to Be," for instance, with Edgar Guest's "A Song" ("None knows the day that friends must part / None knows how near is sorrow . . ."), or put Dylan Thomas' "Do Not Go Gentle into That Good Night" beside Guest's "Failures."

> Do not go gentle into that good night,
> Old age should burn and rave at close of day;
> Rage, rage against the dying of the light.
>
> Though wise men at their end know dark is right,
> Because their words had forked no lightning they
> Do not go gentle into that good night.
>
> Good men, the last wave by, crying how bright
> Their frail deeds might have danced in a green bay,
> Rage, rage against the dying of the light.
>
> Wild men who caught and sang the sun in flight,
> And learn, too late, they grieved it on its way,
> Do not go gentle into that good night.
>
> Grave men, near death, who see with blinding sight
> Blind eyes could blaze like meteors and be gay,
> Rage, rage against the dying of the light.
>
> And you, my father, there on the sad height,
> Curse, bless, me now with your fierce tears, I pray,
> Do not go gentle into that good night.
> Rage, rage against the dying of the light.

At first the students may think the Thomas poem difficult, but if they read it carefully, they will soon come to see that it presents a straightforward, serious subject by means of fresh and symbolic images of light and darkness; that it has a pronounced rhythm, but not a monotonously regular one (note the stresses on "Do not," "Rage, rage," "Curse, bless," and so on); that the sounds in the lines (blind, blaze, be; rave, rage, rage) have appropriate effects; that the tone is a rich complex of attitudes: solemnity, indignation, and grief; in short, that it is a poem that will reward the reader abundantly and repeatedly.

Guest's "Failures," on the other hand, seems at first to be easy and familiar.

> 'Tis better to have tried in vain,
>   Sincerely striving for a goal,
> Than to have lived upon the plain
>   An idle and a timid soul.
>
> 'Tis better to have fought and spent
>   Your courage, missing all applause,
> Than to have lived in smug content
>   And never ventured for a cause.
>
> For he who tries and fails may be
>   The founder of a better day;
> Though never his the victory,
>   From him shall others learn the way.

But as the students read it carefully, they will soon come to see that the basic proposition of the poem, superficially reassuring, is in fact so loose-jointed that it is useless or dangerous (it justifies Hitler as well as Joan of Arc); that the images are dull clichés ("striving for a goal," "lived upon the plain," "learn the way") or impossible to visualize (how does one "found" a "day"?); that the language of the poem is partly archaic ("'Tis") and partly rhetorical ("in vain"); that the tone is smugly Pollyannistic; that the rhythm is monotonously mechanical; and that the sounds are totally random, in no way supporting the sense. It is, in short, a very bad poem.

The teacher may want to avoid such easy marks, however, and choose a bad (or at least mediocre) poem by a good poet. I gather that students often think poets are somehow mysteriously ranked and then uncritically accepted, *in toto*. It might be refreshing for them to know that the same poet who wrote "When Lilacs Last in the Dooryard Bloom'd" could also produce a poem as rhythmically insensitive as "O Captain! My Captain!"; that the author of the magically evocative lines:

> I only hear
> Its melancholy, long, withdrawing roar,
> Retreating, to the breath
> Of the night-wind, down the vast edges drear
> And naked shingles of the world[31]

could also bring himself to write and publish:

> Who prop, thou ask'st, in these bad days, my mind?[32]

and that the inspired hand that wrote

> Rough winds do shake the darling buds of May[33]

was also somehow capable of:

> Those lips that Love's own hand did make
> Breathed forth the sound that said "I hate,"
> To me that languished for her sake[34]

and scores of other lines no better. ("Would he had blotted a thousand" of them, said Ben Jonson.) In fact, it might be a good idea to compare in some detail two sonnets by the greatest of our poets, to show as forcefully as possible that judging a poem should depend upon the merits of the poem itself, not upon the reputation of its author.

The better students may already know Sonnet 73:

> That time of year thou mayst in me behold
> When yellow leaves, or none, or few, do hang
> Upon those boughs which shake against the cold,
> Bare ruin'd choirs, where late the sweet birds sang.
> In me thou see'st the twilight of such day
> As after sunset fadeth in the west;

Which by and by black night doth take away,
Death's second self, that seals up all in rest.
In me thou see'st the glowing of such fire,
That on the ashes of his youth doth lie,
As the death-bed whereon it must expire,
Consumed with that which it was nourish'd by.
    This thou perceiv'st, which makes thy love more strong,
    To love that well which thou must leave ere long.

The virtues of this poem are so obvious that the students will surely see them for themselves: the succession of poignant metaphors, all directing us to the powerful concluding couplet; the clear and pointed imagery of lines 2, 3, 4, 5, 6, 9, and 10; the appropriately solemn movement of the whole poem, especially in the measured emphases of lines 4 and 8 which round off the first two metaphors; and the graceful expression of the whole poem, which makes even the contrived figure in lines 9-12 seem natural and fitting.

Few students, if any, however, will have come across Sonnet 138:

When my love swears that she is made of truth,
I do believe her, though I know she lies,
That she might think me some untutor'd youth,
Unlearned in the world's false subtleties.
Thus vainly thinking that she thinks me young,
Although she knows my days are past the best,
Simply I credit her false-speaking tongue:
On both sides thus is simple truth suppress'd.
But wherefore says she not she is unjust?
And wherefore say not I that I am old?
O, love's best habit is in seeming trust,
And age in love loves not to have years told:
    Therefore I lie with her and she with me,
    And in our faults by lies we flatter'd be.

Here is Shakespeare *manqué*, Shakespeare mechanically doing his duty to a literary convention. The modish and wearying Renaissance preciosity that is never far below the surface in the Sonnets here bobs up again and again: "Vainly thinking that she thinks me young," "Wherefore says she not she is unjust?" "Age in love loves not to have years told," and so on. The general dullness of the poem can be laid chiefly to the prevalence of clichés, both clichés of language and clichés of thought: "untutor'd youth," "the world's false subtleties," "my days are past the best," "her false-speaking tongue." All this is mixed together with a number of thoroughly prosaic lines: "On both sides thus is simple truth suppressed," "Love's best habit is in seeming trust," "I lie with her and she with me." And at the end of the poem, the author—in a hurry to have done with it, perhaps—resorts to an awkward inversion of the word order, to get a concluding rhyme.

The idea of "bad Shakespeare" may be something of a shock treatment for the more conventional students, but it will serve at least two purposes: it should demonstrate that criticism need not be a slave to cults of personality, that even the best poets need to be loved this side idolatry; and it should also demonstrate not only that there are real and usable criteria for judging poems but that one's experience with any poem is in a sense incomplete until these criteria have led the reader, overtly or implicitly, to an esthetic judgment.

·   ·   ·

An exercise that might be useful to the more interested students is a study in some depth of a single period or author. This could include not only a wide reading of the poet or group of poets chosen but also some work with secondary sources: biographies, relevant historical studies, scholarship, and criticism. A special study of this kind might involve some coordination between an English class and a history class or could be usefully undertaken in schools using a core curriculum or team teaching. One way of making such a special study might be to use certain kinds of social poetry as a focus: poetry about politics, say, or poetry by Negroes. One could begin such units of study with anthologies (Arna Bontemps' *American Negro Poetry*, for instance, and Langston Hughes'

New Negro Poets: USA) and then work outward, studying individual poets in some depth.

The danger in this kind of propect is that students may become
so involved in the nonliterary aspects of the study that literature
is sacrificed to sociology, to history, or to something else. If students are not mature enough in the experience of poetry to maintain a literary focus in such work, then it would be better to avoid
it altogether. It is true that a poem can serve as an entrance into
the dense cluster of history and biography from which it proceeds;
but in an English class, the emphasis should always be the other
way around: history and biography should be invoked to sophis-
ticate and enlarge the experience of the poem.

.   .   .

Another special exercise too often scorned, I think, is memorizing.
I do not mean memorizing long poems; many a neutral has been
driven over to the enemy by such assignments. But short lyrics, or
short, key passages of longer poems are worth memorizing. A
teacher hearing a student recite these poems can tell whether or
not he really understands them; the teacher becomes, during the
recitation, the director of a dramatic performance and can operate the way a director does. ("What do you think that line
means?" or "No, what the poet is saying is . . ."). If an actress pronounced "Wherefore art thou Romeo?" as if the "wherefore" meant
"where," instead of "why," the director would interrupt the re-
hearsal. The teacher listening to memory work has the same pedagogical advantage.

It might be dull if everyone in a class memorized all of the same
poems. On the other hand, it is a good idea to have one or two good
poems in common: some of the students will enjoy reciting lines
to each other occasionally; and a few poems thoroughly known
and shared by a whole class serve the useful function of building

a micro-culture based on something other than cliques, clothes, and cars.

. . .

Finally, it might not be a bad idea, toward the end of the unit on poetry, to encourage (but not require) everyone to write a short poem. Some of these could be duplicated and distributed to the class, to be discussed in the same way students have become used to discussing other poems. No one (least of all the teacher) should expect too much from these assigned poems, but some of the results may be surprising. A few of the poems may be good, or at least good in places. A student of mine once wrote, in a successful attempt at imagery, that after falling on the sidewalk, the palm of his hand was "oozing blood like a fresh-cut orange"; this kind of vividness is sometimes available to students precisely because their heads are not yet cluttered with literary clichés. But even if no one in the class writes a very good poem, the mere attempt to do so may lead students to a new respect for successful poems and cause them to think seriously about how a poem really works. That kind of thinking should be valuable to them whenever they read a poem.

. . .

A footnote on examinations: some things, I think, should not be graded. One may ask a student to write out a poem he has memorized, and grade that for accuracy. But one should not grade an oral reading; one should simply try to improve it as much as possible. One may test a student's perception of imagery, but questions about rhythm should perhaps be optional, or otherwise account for the fact that some students cannot help not hearing the rhythms. Examinations should concentrate on the specific qualities that the teacher has been talking and asking about throughout the unit on poetry: the various kinds of meanings, the various kinds of sounds, and tone. One should surely also ask about a poem's total effectiveness: do all of the elements of the poem coalesce in a meaningful whole? The final (ungradable) question is whether the poem has become, for the student, a genuine experience—whether it has compelled that intense participation which—in love or laughter or sorrow or anger—is always, in a poem, the experience of joy.

APPENDIX

Aside from textbooks, there is another way of getting help in the classroom, a way that college professors depend upon as a matter of course: that is, by utilizing the best scholarship and criticism in print. Some of what is published by and for professors is too specialized for use in high school classes, but not all of it. Materials in *The Explicator*, for instance, are often useful for teaching at any level. *Poetry Explication* (Denver, 1962), a book edited by Joseph Kuntz, is a handy and extensive checklist of interpretations of British and American poems. There are also some helpful publications specifically for the use of high school teachers. *The English Journal* runs, as a regular feature, "Poetry in the Classroom," in which teachers describe their teaching experiences with particular poems; the National Council of Teachers of English collected some of these in a 1963 pamphlet called *Modern Poetry in the Classroom*.

As a brief indication of the usefulness of such work, I am appending two analyses of Hopkins' "Spring and Fall" (see the text of the poem on p. 75), one by a high school teacher, the other by a university professor. There are differences in emphasis in the two men's treatments of the poem, but both help to suggest how a teacher might get at the poem in class. The first, an explication by John A. Myers, Jr., teacher of English at the Hun School, Princeton, New Jersey, is entitled "Intimations of Mortality: An Analysis of Hopkins' 'Spring and Fall.'" The essay is included in *Modern Poetry in the Classroom* and is reprinted here by permission of both the writer and the NCTE.

Students are almost always intrigued and often excited by this poem. Even when they do not fully grasp the theme, they respond to the poem's mood and tone; and they are charmed by its simple but powerful music: its sprung rhythms, its sounds (with its skillful use of alliteration and internal rhyme), its fresh and original language. Of course, even without such Hopkins coinages as *unleaving, wanwood,* and *leafmeal,* the poem's language is deceptive: its diction is simple, but individual words are combined in startling ways, are forced to take on new meanings or to compress several possible meanings into themselves. It is this combination of simplicity and compression that teases the student and makes him feel that surely this is a poem he can master, however elusive its central meaning remains. Often he will come to class eager to confirm his own ideas but receptive to the insights toward which the teacher can direct him.

Under these conditions there are many ways of "springing" this poem for a class of eleventh or twelfth graders. I shall suggest one method of presentation which has proved successful. This might be called the thematic approach, but it is heavily dependent on a consideration of the poem's dramatic structure (which emphasizes the relationship of the speaker of the poem to the person spoken to—or about) and a close examination of the poem's language. In fact, this approach will demonstrate, as well as any other, the inseparability of form, language, and meaning in poetry and will enable the teacher to reveal the fallacy of paraphrase.

I like to start with the title, which tells us something about the setting (autumn) and the characters (a child and an older person who is addressing himself to the child) of our drama. It evens tells us something of the poem's theme since it suggests that fall and spring are somehow connected or involved in one another and that there is a further connection between these two seasons and the child—or the child's feelings. All of these matters are tentative at the beginning and must be confirmed by a careful examination of the dramatic situation and the language. We will return to the title later.

Most students can grasp the dramatic situation and can understand the "plot" once they have mastered the second line. The speaker of the poem, a fond and philosophical adult, wonders that Margaret can grieve "over Goldengrove unleaving"—or a grove of trees whose yellow leaves are falling. Some students may have been thrown off by reading *unleaving* as "not leaving" rather than "deleaf-ing!" Once this matter is cleared up, the teacher can proceed rapidly with his examination of the poem. He will, of course, be able to consider many details of language, syntax, sound, and meter that cannot be dealt with in this paper. One such detail might be the capitalization of Goldengrove. Apparently Hopkins wants us to think of this as a *particular* and perhaps favorite grove known to both speaker and child by this name. But the teacher might ask what further tonal effect the poet has achieved by running the two words together.

At this point in the analysis of the role of the speaker, the teacher might ask the vital question, is the speaker actually talking *to* Margaret? A consideration of the kind of speculation the speaker is indulging in makes it clear that he is *not* but is merely musing out loud. The scene has a different meaning for him than it has for Margaret, and Margaret would hardly understand the play of his mind and his emotions. Some support for this interpretation can be gained from an analysis of the rhythm and rhyme of lines three and four. Line three seems to be an example of Hopkins' sprung rhythm. Somehow Hopkins has set up what might be called a dactylic or trochaic expectation for line four, but he surprises us by retaining the accented *you* in line three (compressing the spring, so to speak) and releases us into line four, which begins with an anapest, hovers the accent over *thoughts*, and then reverts to the trochaic pattern with "care for, can you?" "Can you" rhymes with "man, you," but it has a different beat, and the tension created by this conflict between rhyme and meter serves to emphasize the *rhetorical* nature of the question. The forced accent on *you* makes this a pivotal word, and the total effect of these two lines is to make a sharp differentiation between the speaker with *his* thoughts and the child with *hers*.

We can say, then, it is *as if* the speaker were addressing Margaret as he observes her weeping; and this dramatic fact accounts, in part, for the tone of tenderness and wistfulness that runs throughout the poem. He muses sadly (Ah!) that although Margaret (with her *fresh* thoughts, so like the leaves when they were green) can care for leaves as if they were human ("like the things of man"), the time will come (when the heart, now in its springtime, grows colder) when she will be unmoved by such a phenomenon even though it will be witnessed on a much vaster scale and when the process has gone much further ("Worlds of wanwood leafmeal lie"). At this point teachers should invite comments from their students on the possible meanings of *wanwood* and *leafmeal*. These words hold a legitimate fascination for students; teachers can capitalize on the students' love of word games and make of their guesses an exercise in intellectual responsibility. For whatever they find in these words must fit the context of the poem. *Wanwood*, I take to be a compounding of "wan," with its suggestion of the pallor of dead leaves and the sadness of the forest with its completely bare trees (possibly combined with the older meaning "dark," "livid"), and "wormwood" with its suggestion of the human counterpart in bitterness and disappointment. *Leafmeal* seems compounded of "piecemeal," the slow attrition of nature, and "leafmould," suggestive of utter decay.

What does line 9 signify? Does it say that Margaret *insists* on weeping and in demanding an answer? Or does it mean that Margaret will weep even when she is an adult, only then she will *know* why she weeps? Or both? I leave this ambiguity to the reader though I think my preference will emerge shortly.

Now, in line 10, contains a similar and related ambiguity. Is it simply an indication of present time, or is it the sound one makes to comfort a child ("Now, now, child")? In either case, Margaret the child should not concern herself with the *name* or the secret cause of the sorrow that she has "guessed" intuitively. After all, the sources or "springs" (ask your students how many valid meanings they can find in this word; check especially for *sorrow's springtimes*) of sorrow are the same—the same for adult or child—whether they have been articulated, consciously understood ("mouth had") or only intuited ("heart heard of, ghost guessed"— the student may need some explanation here of *ghost as spirit* and can be reminded of Holy Ghost). Margaret will know the name of her sorrow all too soon.

The last two lines announce what the entire poem has been building toward, the tragic fact that Margaret has guessed at and that is symbolized for her by the falling leaves. The *blight* to be suffered by the golden grove is the blight common to all mankind and implicit in his being born—*just as autumn is implicit in spring*. But what exactly *is* this blight? At this point everything depends on our interpretation of the enigmatic and climactic last line. Without knowing it, Margaret is mourning for herself. What does this mean? And why is her plight identified with that of mankind? It is too easy to say that this blight is death—mere physical destruction—and that Margaret has somehow recognized in the death of nature an emblem of the mortality which includes her. This is only part of the meaning, for what Margaret senses must die is not so much Margaret the person as *Margaret the child*. And what the adult speaker is most keenly aware of is the inevitable loss of childhood innocence with its sense of perfection and immortality. Consciousness of death is also consciousness of human limitation and imperfection and the acceptance of these: it is consciousness of sin.

The adult will weep and *know* that he is weeping for his "childhood's faith," that "sweet golden clime" where everything was perfect and everything was possible. We return to the title. This is not a poem about fall alone; it is a poem about spring *and* fall. Is it too much to suggest that it is about innocence and the fall from innocence?

The following analysis is excerpted from Irvin Ehrenpresis, "Why Literature Should Be Taught," *Proceedings of the Philosophy of Education Society* (1958), pp. 100-102.

Who is speaking in the poem? What can you tell about him as a person, from his tone? Clearly, he is a grown man, perhaps elderly, who has endured enough sadness to know that human life is darkly colored by tragic ingredients. To whom is he speaking? We see that it must be a little girl unaccustomed to pain. What is the occasion? The child is weeping because autumn has come; she feels unhappy to see a grove of trees stripped of the foliage which made them beautiful. Within this dramatic setting, the man speaks.

Does she hear his message? No, the language is certainly not the sort that a child could follow. The man addresses her silently. From the meaning of his speech, we may suspect that he is also addressing his younger self, with whom he identifies the girl. By implication, therefore, we may take it that his commentary is meant to apply to the whole span of human experience. The poet thus gives form to a mood which every person feels as he comes to acknowledge that certain unbearable miseries are inseparable from existence. I do not assert that this mood is universally and eternally valid; I assert only that it is an authentic part of all men's character at moments of tragic insight. The dramatic pattern therefore encloses an emotional symbol which is the speaker's remark to the girl. The poem does not consist of that message; it consists of the situation as giving rise to the message, and the whole drama as standing for a dynamic aspect of the poet's personality—an aspect which seems connotative and evocative because the poet implies that any understanding reader will find it analogous to similar rhythms in his own character.

Through his speech the man says that the girl's suffering is ironic. She cannot understand how grief and pain may belong to a world which otherwise seems satisfactory. Yet when she has grown up, and learned to accept suffering as a natural part of living, she will regard her present despair as trivial. So the poet makes a rhetorical pattern of the message: as innocence ripens into knowledge, short miseries grow into permanent sorrow. She does not know *why* now; and now the pain will quickly pass. She will know *why* as an adult; but then the pain will be permanent. The appeal of the poem does not depend upon the truth of this teaching, but on its evocative embodiment of an authentic mood: i.e., whether or not we all believe that life is a tragedy, we all have moods when life seems a tragedy; and the author has composed his rhetorical design out of this fact.

He has also found a sensuous pattern of imagery analogous to the other movements of the poem. The passage of the seasons from summer to fall, the turning of leaves from green to gold to withered, the visual flow of the dropping foliage stripping the trees naked, all reflect the current of human life from infancy to age, and of human moods from infant laughter to elderly despair. The inevitability of seasonal transitions invites us to accept the human changes with resignation.

The individual words play upon the other designs. By giving the grove a proper name, the poet suggests the child's animistic attitude. Through his coinages—"unleaving," "wanwood," "leaf-meal"—and through his unexpected interpretations of familiar words—"springs" for origins, "ghost" for soul, "blight" for doom—he shocks us into attention; and yet these words are not so odd as to disturb the solemnity of the poem in general. They are all simple and of Anglo-Saxon derivation, giving the expressions the effect of proverbial wisdom.

The sounds of the poem add other designs to those which I have analyzed. Merely by repeating the child's name at the beginning and end (but nowhere else), the poet ties the whole together. In both these lines he reinforces the effect by alliteration and assonance. In the first line the "ar" sounds of *Margaret* are echoed in the verb *are*; the "gr" combination is echoed in *grieving*. In the last line the "mr" combination is repeated in *mourn*. Such arabesques of sound give the lyric a flowing and unified concord which enhances the other patterns. Every line has some musical but not too emphatic resonance of this sort; and in places such contrasts and similarities appear to have special meanings: the richness of "over Goldengrove" switches into the sharp vowel of "unleaving," as if to hint at the change from August to November. The "sameness" of all "sorrow's springs" is suggested by the repeated sibilants in that line; and in the following line, the parallelism between "mind" and "mouth" is borne out by the "m's."

Beneath the patterns of drama, rhetoric, sense, imagery, language, and sound, beats the meter of the poem. It is an unusual rhythm, having four accents to the line; half the lines end with an unaccented syllable; and each line has a total of six to eight syllables. Some accents are marked by the poet because he wishes them to be set in rather unusual positions. The result of these details is to make the poem structurally original in a way that would be apparent to an experienced reader. Yet they do not interrupt the normal word order of a sentence and they do not sound irritatingly obtrusive. While the meter is fresh, it is also deliberate, for the phrases advance in a dignified, slow step which belongs to their somber implications. The trailing effect of ending with unaccented syllables, rather than the clipped style of ordinary iambic meters, carries through the brooding manner of the whole little work. There are, as well, units which underline syntactical parallelisms, such as the beats falling on "come" and "colder," or "spare" and "sigh," or "mouth" and "mind." Elsewhere, the accent clarifies the sense, as in "you *will* weep" or the rush of "Nor mouth had, no nor *mind*, expressed." The rhythm of the last line reaches an appropriate crest in *Margaret* and then falls away: "It is Margaret you mourn for."

Most comprehensively, there are the possibilities of larger symbolism; e.g., in the title. *Spring* obviously is the child; *fall* obviously is the older man. But from the tragic overtones of the poet's morality, we may suspect that *spring* is also the springing time of innocent life; *fall*, the decaying time of fallen humanity; the wood or garden setting may have connotations of Eden; the nostalgia may refer not only to the naïveté of childhood but to the purity of Man before his Biblical "Fall" from grace. I shall not insist on this sort of allusion; yet it sticks in the mind of a careful reader. . . .

NOTES

1. T. S. Eliot, *The Waste Land.*
2. Ezra Pound, *Canto I.*
3. Dylan Thomas, "Altarwise by Owl-light."
4. Dylan Thomas, "Poem in October."
5. Howard Nemerov, *Poets on Poetry* (Chicago, 1966), p. 240.
6. *Beowulf*, lines 813-818, trans. Lucien Dean Pearson (Bloomington, Ind., 1965), p. 59.
7. Robert Frost, "To Earthward."
8. Wilfred Owen, *"Dulce et Decorum Est."*
9. John Crowe Ransom, "Here Lies a Lady."
10. Archibald MacLeish, *"Ars Poetica."*
11. William Wordsworth, "Upon Westminster Bridge."
12. Edwin Arlington Robinson, "Mr. Flood's Party."
13. Michael Drayton, "Since There's No Help."
14. William Shakespeare, Sonnet 73.
15. Andrew Marvell, "Bermudas."
16. Samuel Taylor Coleridge, "Kubla Khan."
17. John Keats, "To Autumn."
18. Alfred Lord Tennyson, "The Lotos-Eaters."
19. Robert Browning, "Meeting at Night."
20. Philip Larkin, "Toads."
21. Richard Wilbur, "A Simile for her Smile."
22. Wilfred Owen, "Anthem for Doomed Youth."
23. William Carlos Williams, "The Red Wheelbarrow."
24. e. e. cummings, "Portrait VIII."
25. William Shakespeare, Sonnet 30.
26. John Milton, "On His Deceased Wife."
27. William Wordsworth, "England, 1802."
28. Alfred Lord Tennyson, "Morte d'Arthur."
29. Alfred Lord Tennyson, "Sweet and Low."

30. Howard Nemerov, "The View from an Attic Window."
31. Matthew Arnold, "Dover Beach."
32. Matthew Arnold, "To a Friend."
33. William Shakespeare, Sonnet 18.
34. William Shakespeare, Sonnet 145.

5

On Teaching Drama

GERALD RABKIN

Associate Professor of English,
Indiana University

We read plays and we see them performed. They exist in books, fixed with the immobility of the printed word. Drama represents, then, a prime constituent of our literary tradition. The first great work of literary criticism is, after all, a work of dramatic criticism. But just as Aristotle theorized a century after the great outburst of Attic creativity, abstracting principles of tragic response from what had been the evolving practice of a living, changing drama, the literary history of dramatic expression is more often than not the rationalizing of stage popularity. Drama is a tyrannously popular art; while cases do exist of initially unpopular works finding later audiences, on the whole the very nature of drama ties it much more stringently than poetry or fiction to immediate collective approval. Drama is literature, but it is something more. With crucial exceptions, the history of drama as a literary form is very largely the history of those works which have survived *on stage*.

Drama is the most "impure" of the three major literary genres; its very form derives from this "impurity." I of course use "impurity" metaphorically, for purity is as spurious a concept in esthetics as in linguistics or ethnogeny. What I mean to assert is that the form of drama reveals a necessary dependence upon the other arts. We can read a play as though it were intended for the printed page, but in so doing we partially falsify it, for insofar as it survives as "real" rather than "closet" drama its esthetic success is dependent upon its theatrical viability. Thus, in reading a play we must be aware that we are not accepting it fully on its own terms. Unlike poetry or fiction, drama interposes a series of inter-pretative artists—director, actor, scenic designer, musician—be-tween the writer and his audience. We may imaginatively fill those gaps in the act of reading, but we must acknowledge their existence. We can, after all, if we acquire the skill, learn to read a printed musical score, but we do not confuse this experience with a full concert experience. Similarly, the experience of reading a play to a great extent represents an imaginative substitute for theatrical performance.

And yet I think it fallacious to assert that the play can be appre-ciated fully *only* in its theatrical context. In art, as in all things, the Emersonian Law of Compensation applies: if the playwright's dramatic vision can be enhanced by his theatrical collaborators, it can also be destroyed by them. I recall one of my English pro-fessors in graduate school who resolutely refused to see Shake-speare performed because no actors nor designers could possibly approach the grandeur created in his mind's eye in the privacy of his study. To some extent he was justified. The theatrical experi-ence is a concrete one: it embodies action in a continuous present. We watch *this* specific *Hamlet* at *this* specific time in *this* specific theatre. Our imagination clothes the text in less palpable form. The Hamlet which our imagination creates now inevitably differs from the Hamlet we created in our school days. But no physical presence is thrust before our eyes to jolt us to this recognition. It is prob-ably better, therefore, to read a play well than attend a mediocre performance (unless we are particularly skilled in learning from bad examples). The solitary act of reading permits us to savor the text at our own speed. As with a novel we can dwell upon passages, refresh our memories as to plot and character, enjoy a concentration born of our own pace—all without the tyranny of the headlong rush of physical performance.

All this we can and should do. And yet if we demand no more of drama we are playing false with it. For if theatrical mediocrity can degrade a great play, theatrical brilliance can elevate an inferior one. In drama we must continually acknowledge the creative contribution of the interpretative artist. It is his task to transmit the playwright's vision to us. In fiction and poetry we confront the literary text directly, but in drama the confrontation is less direct. The interpretative artists may fail, but when they succeed they enhance the playwright's creative imagination with their own. The ideal conjunction of great performance and great play only too infrequently occurs; when it does, however, drama reaches a height unattainable by the other literary genres. As Eric Bentley writes in *The Life of the Drama*:

> . . . for anyone capable of relishing theatre—and that includes more people than know it—even though the written script has its own completeness, there is no pleasure to top that of seeing a dramatic masterpiece masterfully performed. What is added means so much in such an immediate, sensuous way. If plot, characterization and dialogue give body to the theme, and transform thought into wisdom, and a view into a vision, adequate performance helps them to do so in various ways but above all by adding that final and conclusive concretion, the living actor (p. 149).

Like the legendary phoenix, theatrical tradition is replenished by the embers of past performances. The novel, the poem remain fixed; the consciousness of their readers changes. But the drama must continually *absorb* the consciousness of its age. The strength of drama is its very literary incompleteness. We can only surmise what Richard Burbage brought to Hamlet or Othello; the actor's art is necessarily ephemeral (at least until the advent of the motion picture). But inasmuch as it is drama meant for performance, Shakespeare's work assumes the necessity of this transient contribution. As a consummate man of the theatre, Shakespeare created not only great *characters* but great *roles*. His unbroken command of our literary tradition is paralleled by his unbroken command of our theatrical tradition. Even when bowdlerized or rewritten, his plays have dominated the living stage. In one tone or another Shakespeare's living voice has spoken to successive generations.

There can be, then, no definitive "edition" of a theatrical performance, no matter how impressive, for every age must create the play anew literally in its own image. After Laurence Olivier's magnificent film version of *Henry V*, the critics asked how it would be possible to achieve a more perfect realization of the play. But Olivier's heroic portrayal, the product of a nation at war, has given way recently to less patriotic, even anti-heroic characterizations. Similarly, Peter Brooks' great recent production of *King Lear* could have emerged only in an age that has produced both Samuel Beckett's *Endgame* and Peter Weiss' *Marat/Sade*. Far from falsifying Shakespeare, these new productions affirm his continued greatness. If, as Professor Jan Kott demonstrates in his recent book, Shakespeare is indeed our contemporary, in the theatre we meet him man to man.

Thus, the literature vs. theatre debate is essentially a false one, to a large extent (in America at least) the result of the unfortunate parceling out of drama between literature and theatre departments in universities. Each group, therefore, has a vested interest in establishing its bona fides. The *littérateurs* assert the common grounds that drama shares with the other literary genres; the theatre people assert its uniqueness, the inseparability of play and performance. Each group, as Eric Bentley points out, tries to make a virtue of its own "*déformation professionnelle*." Writers on drama tend to overstress either its literary or its theatrical elements. Professional literary critics distrust the dramatic genre, preferring instead poetry or fiction, and professional newspaper and periodical drama reviewers, with one or two crucial exceptions, often have no literary credentials whatsoever. All this is unfortunate because both orientations are vital. As can be seen from what I have previously written, I feel strongly that the conventions of drama are rooted in their theatrical origins. And yet, once established, literary conventions tend to perpetuate themselves in a traditionally literary manner. The play *does* exist as a literary manifestation because it is treated as such. But insofar as these conventions ultimately derive from theatrical necessity, even a purely literary reading of a dramatic text must confront theatrical values, as Harley Granville-Barker, for example, pointed out in his significant reinterpretations of Shakespearean drama earlier in the century.

DRAMA, CONVENTION, AND REALITY

In teaching or discussing drama it seems to me particularly important to consider the role of artistic conventions in determining esthetic form. For, as we have indicated, drama, because of its dual literary and theatrical existence, represents the most conventional of traditional literary genres. One perennial problem that teachers of literature must face is the student's confusion of art and life. Literary characters—and particularly dramatic characters—are treated as though they were real people in the real world. (Literary critics for a long time made the same mistake with Hamlet.) The student finds it difficult to recognize that a character in a farce or in a high tragedy is not meant to function in the same manner as a character in a naturalistic play. The tendency is to equate "realism" with esthetic success: "this character/play/scene is good because it's like real life." The confusion in drama is particularly acute because drama is meant to be embodied by "real" actors on a "real" stage. Moreover, since Ibsen—and despite attempts to reverse the trend—the major impetus of modern drama has been "realistic," that is, the representation of the *illusion* of reality on the stage. The motion picture and television—the mass media through which most people confront some species of drama at present—similarly contribute to the acceptance of realism as the sole legitimate dramatic mode.

It is necessary, therefore, for the teacher of drama to point out to his students that all art involves the acceptance of conventions, however these conventions may differ, and that *realism itself is a convention.* This can be indicated in several ways: all students, for example, accept the basic conventions of the motion picture; no one finds anything startling in being confronted by an immense close-up of the face of an actor on the screen. And yet, when the great film pioneer D. W. Griffith originally exploited the use of the close-up in such early films as *The Birth of a Nation* and *Intolerance,* critics derisively complained that audiences would never accept a disembodied head or hand floating imperiously in the darkness of the cinema theatre. The *convention* in films, until Griffith began expanding the cinema's vocabulary, was to shoot all scenes in medium long shot so that the actor's entire body was constantly visible as on stage. In moving the camera close to his subject to isolate some significant detail, Griffith broke away from the tyranny of the theatre's fixed point of view and helped establish a new convention based upon the unique capabilities of the cinema.

Even in the naturalistic theatre, in which fidelity to observable reality is most acute, we accept many conventions which "violate" the real world. We accept the convention that furniture in a realistic box set is placed around the edges of the set but not downstage along the invisible fourth wall, whose "invisibility" we also accept. We accept the convention that actors "project" so that their lines are audible; we accept the convention that they move and stand in such a way that they do not "block" each other, so that the audience's view of the stage action remains unimpaired. And in addition to these theatrical conventions, a naturalistic play involves certain literary assumptions: that no matter how accurate a "slice of life" is presented, reality may be so condensed, ordered, and structured that esthetic form can be achieved within severe limitations of time. In this regard drama imposes much severer restraints upon the writer than the novel. The naturalistic novels can (and did, as the mammoth works of the late nineteenth and early twentieth centuries indicate) exhaustively recreate the complex texture of the real world by the gradual accretion of detail. In length, the novel is open-ended, and the novelist has world enough and time to create painstakingly (indeed, sometimes to the infinite boredom of his readers) a minutely detailed portrait of the world he has chosen to describe.

The conventions of drama prevent so exhaustive a presentation, for the fact of theatrical performance demands that the playwright work within a relatively fixed time span. Western audiences have rarely been able to equal the stamina of the Chinese playgoer, who apparently can watch day-long plays with little diminution of attention—although the viewers of Greek trilogies and medieval mystery cycles obviously had more staying power than contemporary audiences (unless narcotized by television). Playwrights like O'Neill have striven to break the tyranny of the two-hour traffic of the stage with varied results. If the play is good, we watch; but these experiments have not succeeded in effectively lengthening the attention span of the average audience.

Realism, then, is itself a convention: it makes certain assumptions about the way the artist looks at the world and the means he chooses to transcribe it. This point must be forcefully asserted: realism does *not* represent the summit of artistic achievement, but rather one of several esthetic approaches, and in drama a relatively new one. Insofar as the term is defined with sufficient specificity to be meaningful, it refers to the attempt to apply to art the philosophical assumption which emerges with Descartes and Locke in the seventeenth and eighteenth centuries that the particulars of experience can be meaningfully examined apart from a given body of traditional, universal beliefs. The novel, which emerges as a dominant form in the eighteenth century, takes as its primary criterion the assumption that the writer's essential task is to deal with the truth of individual experience, which is always unique, unprecedented, new—hence *novel*.

In the drama, inevitably governed by time lag because of its dependence upon popular response, the impact of realistic theory is not felt until the end of the nineteenth century, a period of intense intellectual probing and social change. The pioneers of modern drama—Ibsen, Strindberg, Hauptmann, Chekhov—preoccupied with the vital ideological and social issues of their day, felt, in varying ways, the need to confront reality as it *was*, not through what they felt was the haze of romantic conventions. They wanted a drama *and* a theatre (the one presupposed or demanded the other) which would not, in their view, palliate the hypocrisies, absurdities, and injustices of the real world. As Constantine Stanislavski, the great Russian director, asserted: "We protested against the old manner of acting, against theatricalism, false pathos, declamation, artificiality . . . , bad staging, the emphasis on new productions that spoiled the ensemble work, the whole system of presentations, and the insignificant repertoires of the time."

Not surprisingly, the new drama demanded this new concept of a Theatre (the capital is significant: a Theatre represented not only a playhouse, but the entire set of values, esthetic and humanist, which united the theatrical artists). The plays of Ibsen and Chekhov could not be produced in the vast, cavernous, Grand Opera structures into which theatres had evolved by the mid-nineteenth century. Small, intimate theatres suitable for believable, nondeclamatory acting and accurate, scale representations of settings had to emerge to service the dramatic needs of the new playwrights. And so they did: the Théâtre Libre in France, the Independent Theatre in England, the Freie Bühne in Germany, and, later, the Washington Square Players and Provincetown Players in America. A great percentage of significant modern drama is directly indebted to the existence of these "little" theatres.

But yesterday's avant-garde becomes today's establishment. It must be noted that by no means were these theatres, nor the playwrights who wrote for them, totally committed to the production of realistic plays. Significantly, the work of Ibsen and Strindberg, and later O'Neill in our country, moves increasingly away from realistic assumptions: the naturalism of *A Doll's House, Miss Julie,* and *Beyond the Horizon* is superseded by the experimentalism of *When We Dead Awaken, The Dream Play,* and *The Great God Brown.* The conventions of realism present their own severe limitations. It is paradoxical that realism should become so established as the dominant dramatic mode of our time, because no playwrights more clearly recognized its limitations than its original champions. O'Neill, as a conscious heir of Strindberg, throughout his long and prolific career continually endeavored to expand the conventions of drama, to stretch the borders of what was possible in the theatre. He experimented boldly, as we have noted, in varying the length of his plays: both *Strange Interlude* and *Mourning Becomes Electra* take between five and six hours to perform. *A Long Day's Journey Into Night* and *The Iceman Cometh* are similarly longer than conventional plays. But O'Neill experimented with more than length: in an attempt to create a "Theatre of Tomorrow" from what had become the stodgy realism of his day, he consciously returned to the nonrealistic conventions of the dramatic tradition to reinstate the chorus, the mask, the soliloquy, and to draw, as the great tragedians of the past did, upon the riches of myth and legend. He recognized, as the insatiable experimentation of his work demonstrates, that the history of drama is *not* essentially the history of the conventions of realism.

The student must be made to recognize, therefore, that the history of dramatic realism represents a tiny fraction of our dramatic heritage, that prose is not the sole linguistic tool of the playwright, that, in fact, our greatest dramatists have often been simultaneously our greatest poets, that once understood the conventions of nonrealistic drama present no more inherent difficulties than the conventions of realism.

DRAMA AND THEATRE

How do we make these dramatic conventions comprehensible? First of all, I feel, through the conventions of theatre which determine them. A good beginning might be to dispense with the ambiguous term "realism" altogether until the student is able to handle it meaningfully. I would suggest the substitution of one or both of the following pairs of antithetical terms: illusionism/non-illusionism, or representationalism/presentationalism. In the illusionistic or representational (i.e., realistic) both play and performance combine to represent the illusion of reality: the language of the play is prose, the language of everyday life; the playwright attempts to portray individualized characters behaving in conformity with our apprehension of how real people behave; he places them in a specified accurately defined milieu which records rather than distorts reality; he is concerned with all detail which will contribute to our belief in the reality of the specific historical and social moment which he is describing. The theatrical artists work to translate the dramatist's approach into actuality: settings are accurate reproductions of the environment of the characters; lighting attempts to transmit the reality of natural or artificial light; the actors, rejecting theatrical grandiloquence, try to create characters who behave just the way real people do in the real world (always excepting the concessions made to visibility and audibility).

In the nonillusionistic or presentational theatre—by far the dominant mode of our theatrical heritage—play and performance make no attempt to disguise themselves, to deny that a play is being performed in a theatre. In the illusionistic theatre, the actors must not acknowledge the audience (except imperceptibly to determine pace and response). To do so would violate the illusion they are striving to create. The proscenium arch rigidly separates the performance from the audience. In the nonillusionistic theatre, however, the actor often acknowledges the audience by talking directly to it and by "aside" confidences to it from time to time. He is by no means constrained—indeed, quite the reverse—to behave as a real person does. Similarly, it is not necessary to place him in a realistically accurate stage environment. The conventions of theatrical settings have varied considerably throughout dramatic history. In the great ages of dramatic creativity in fifth-century Greece and Elizabethan England, for example, scenic effects were minimal by contemporary standards. The theatres themselves served as the basic setting; controlled lighting was nonexistent as both were open-air theatres which depended upon natural light. What might seem, therefore, to a modern playgoer an enormous technical disadvantage in fact had quite the contrary result. The playwrights had to create with words what other more scenically oriented theatres could create with theatrical effect. The great poetic imagery of Aeschylus and Shakespeare represents, therefore, the fortuitous necessity of the playwrights' having to provide what the scenic conventions of their theatres deemed it unnecessary to provide. Indeed, at the risk of hazarding an enormously broad generalization, one might note that throughout dramatic history the greater the concentration on theatrical spectacle and effect the less impressive the dramatic contribution. When spectacle dominates, as in Renaissance Italy, eighteenth-century England, or in Hollywood costume epics of today, all creative energy seems to be spent in contriving theatrical effects, and little is directed toward the artistic success of the play which the effects are theoretically meant to serve.

In the nonillusionistic theatre, therefore, reality is "presented" rather than "represented." The playwright not only accepts the conventions of his theatre, but often exploits them. Shakespeare, for example, was continually open to the possibilities of the conventions of his theatre. The comic entanglements in such plays as *Twelfth Night* and *As You Like It,* which result from the disguise of a girl as a boy, no doubt largely derive from the very nonrealistic fact that on the Elizabethan stage female roles were played by boys. It may also be noted that when Shakespeare's company moves into the theatrically more elaborate confines of the Black-friars theatre, he takes advantage of the additional resources at his command, as the masque in *The Tempest* demonstrates.

Thus, the rich conventions of the Elizabethan theatre—above all a popular theatre—must be understood if the form of Elizabethan drama is to be appreciated. In recent years, producers of Shake-spearean drama have consistently rejected the confines of the proscenium arch, returning instead to a re-creation or an approx-imation of the versatility of the open Elizabethan thrust stage. In this regard, it seems vital to me that students have some awareness of the structure of the Elizabethan playhouse, for it differs radically from their proscenium-oriented view of what a theatre is like. They should be made aware of the many stage areas the playhouse con-tained: the forestage, the inner and upper stages. They should be aware that the playhouse permitted a continual flow of stage action from one scene to the next much in the fluid manner of the cinema, that the stage and act divisions which most texts continue to follow for the sake of convenience are, in fact, later scholarly emendations in the name of classical tradition; that far from being diffuse or episodic, the structure of Elizabethan drama is admir-ably suited to the conventions of the theatre for which it was written.

Although I am not usually an enthusiast for visual aids—I believe that the personal presence of a vital instructor is worth a thousand educational films—I *do* endorse the use of any aids—models, films, drawings—which can bring before the student the concrete image of the physical playhouse of any period. The differences of dra-matic structure in, say, *Oedipus Rex* and *Hamlet* can be commu-nicated vividly if the images of the theatres in which each play was performed are visually presented. If the Elizabethan play-house violates the student's idea of what a theatre is like, the Greek theatre represents even more of a departure from his expectations.

To be aware that Greek drama was performed in a huge, open-air ampitheatric structure which seated more than 15,000 people, more approximate to a sports stadium than to a traditional proscenium theatre, not only permits the student to imaginatively recreate a Greek play in its original setting, but also helps communicate the vital role that drama played in the life of the entire community of the Greek city-state. From a description of the parts of the theatre —the names of which form our basic theatrical vocabulary to this day: the orchestra, the theatron, the skene, etc.—the teacher can move to other theatrical conventions which determine the form of Greek tragedy: the masked and booted actor, a figure larger than life as demanded by the mythic role he must perform; the chorus, on stage almost throughout the entire play, witnessing, commenting, and participating in the rituals of heroism and catastrophe carved by Aeschylus, Sophocles, and Euripides from their rich heritage of legend and myth.

The very role of myth in Greek drama can be fruitfully pursued. We live now in the age of the cult of originality, the "new thing" in art as well as in life. A melodrama-oriented generation feels cheated if it is not presented with the surprise ending or the sudden twist of plot. Through the Greek—and Elizabethan—experience, the student can be made to realize that "originality" in plot does not represent the supreme esthetic achievement, that the great Greek playwrights—and Shakespeare, to a great extent—used familiar, traditional subject matter. The audience largely knew what was going to happen; what mattered was what Euripides brought to the subject as compared to Aeschylus or Sophocles. All three playwrights, for example, wrote very different plays on the Orestes-Electra myth. Attention can then be riveted on dramatic essentials: theme, character, language, plot as the means of developing the former two. It is for this reason that so many contemporary dramatists—Eliot, O'Neill, Sartre, Giraudoux, to name a few—have consciously returned to traditional mythic subject matter. Originality as an artistic desideratum is a relatively late, post-eighteenth-century phenomenon. Before that time the word "original" denoted "first" or "from the origin." "Original sin" was not viewed as a fascinating new perversion.

Familiarity with theatrical conventions can serve, therefore, to help the student appreciate the great range of dramatic expression. It goes without saying that the very best visual aid available is the theatrical performance itself. No greater opportunity exists for the teacher of drama than when his students have the opportunity to see a play which is being studied in performance. The realities of transferring the play into theatrical actuality force the student to compare his imaginative reconstruction of the script with that of the theatre artists. If he is seeing a classic play in a prosecenium theatre, he will have to judge how effectively the producer has found workable equivalents for the traditional conventions. Indeed, even if the student is fortunate enough to see such a play produced on a nonproscenium thrust stage (alas, a not too likely possibility), he will observe what techniques are employed to communicate the play to a contemporary audience. The point cannot be overstressed: if the greatness of art is defined by its power to speak across the ages, the particular glory of the drama consists in the necessity of listening to the voice of this greatness in the accents of the present.

THE FORMS OF DRAMA

We have spoken of the necessity of understanding the varied conventions which underlie the drama of different periods. But in looking over the great range of dramatic expression, we observe that although there exist great differences in form and style, there also exist broad patterns of similarity; the forms of drama have been remarkably persistent through the ages. Although the forms of *Oedipus* and *Hamlet* vary greatly, both were called "tragedies" by their contemporaries, and subsequent generations have found in them, despite their enormous formal dissimilarity, equivalent visions of dramatic grandeur. Tragedy represents, by common assent, the highest form of dramatic achievement, and generations of critics from Aristotle to the present have labored to anatomize its salient characteristics. Our task is more difficult than that of Aristotle, who was, after all, confronting a coherent if varied body of work (not that anyone has done any better), for in our general theory of tragedy we must assimilate the very different achievements of Sophocles, Shakespeare, and Racine—and perhaps Ibsen, O'Neill, and Brecht. The problem of defining tragedy is particularly difficult because the term has been used historically to mean quite dissimilar things. On one hand, as we have observed, tragedy is defined as the supreme dramatic achievement. *Oedipus, Lear, Prédre* become the touchstones by which we measure serious dramatic expression. In this sense "tragedy" is used not as a descriptive concept but as an approbative one. It is almost as though the adjective "great" silently prefaced every utterance of the word. By this criterion, even works which in their own times were called tragedies fail to reach the mark. Euripides' *Iphigeneia in Taurus* and Beaumont and Fletcher's *Maid's Tragedy* are viewed by most critics as failing to achieve the magnificence of "true" tragedy.

These difficulties arise because "tragedy" was used, in periods when the genre flourished, largely as a descriptive term. The Greeks rigidly distinguished between tragedy and comedy, but they permitted wide variation, within established conventions, in what was possible in the former. Contrary to popular notion, Greek tragedy does not inevitably end in catastrophe, as the deification of Oedipus in *Oedipus at Colonus* and the exoneration of Arestes in *The Eumenides* indicate. In Elizabethan drama, however, continuing medieval tradition, tragedy and comedy were defined almost solely in terms of final outcome. *Measure for Measure*, one of Shakespeare's darkest plays, is called a comedy because it ends "happily," as the Duke's intervention sets matters aright; *The Maid's Tragedy,* which ends in catastrophe, is tragic in the broader sense in title alone. Let us remember that the greatest work of the

Middle Ages, one of ultimate seriousness and totally devoid of frivolity, was called by its creator "The Comedy" and by subsequent ages "Divine" because it moves from the horror and misery of Hell to the glory of Paradise, the happiest of all endings for the Christian soul.

Must, then, all attempts at defining tragedy fail? Can we, despite the different uses of the term, find certain common features which bind together the most serious products of dramatic genius? In provisional and general terms I think we can; I have pointed out the ambiguities inherent in the concept in order to warn against the treacherousness of any oversimplified "grand theory." We must not commit the neoclassical fallacy of demanding that tragedy conform to a rigid preconceived formal pattern. We must not deify the pronouncements of Aristotle, as great as they are, or we are apt to fall into the kind of absurdity which makes Corneille have his hero in *Le Cid* declare his love, fight his first duel, kill his sweetheart's father, repel in a tremendous battle a national invasion, win a trial by combat, and in the course of all this, lose and regain the favors of his king and the lady of his heart—all within twenty-four hours in order to conform to the dictates of the unity of action. Above all, we must recognize that if an artistic form is alive it will continually change. The only fixed forms, like languages, are dead ones. Is *Ulysses* a novel? Not by Dickensian standards. Is *Le Sacre du Printemps* music? Not by the standards of Bach. Both Joyce and Stravinsky expanded the possibilities of the art forms in which they were engaged, and hence succeeded in redefining them.

Similarly, Brecht's *Mother Courage* and Lorca's *House of Bernarda Alba* and O'Neill's *Long Day's Journey Into Night* keep the spirit of tragedy alive not by a conscious duplication of past formal structures, but by a grasping of something far less definable: our awareness of the common experience of man through the centuries, our apprehension that certain artists have been able to put on the stage a microcosm of man's despair and exaltation, our assumption that the spectacle of his anguish is humanly significant.

The great tragedies reveal different and yet similar confrontations of man and the implacable forces of the cosmos, however these forces be defined: as fate, society, perhaps even man's own inner contradictions. Indeed, the confrontation must be redefined perennially if it is to remain vital. Attempts to achieve tragedy status by the mere imitation of past forms are doomed to failure; we can duplicate the structure of Chartres but not its spirit. Dryden could not make the style of French neoclassical tragedy viable within the English romantic tradition, nor could Maxwell Anderson re-create Shakespeare's tragic spirit by imitating the form and language of Elizabethan drama. Universality in art can rarely be achieved by consciously striving for it.

If this discussion seems vague and imprecise, it is, I think, the best we can do without falsification. The teacher of drama must guard against any absolute, categorical definition of tragedy. Indeed, for beginning students it may well be advisable not to advance beyond historical definition. The teacher should concentrate on the specifics of the play: theme, plot, character, language, structure. If the student understands the play we can ask little more; we should not attempt to force him into realms of esthetic theory which few scholars or critics have themselves agreed upon.

The problem in comedy is less ambiguous, for in this form we face a more specific human commonality: the capacity to laugh at absurdity. Despite the medieval and Renaissance attempt to define comedy in terms of outcome rather than effect, the great universal of comic expression has been the healing sound of human laughter. Why we laugh is a complex and disputed point: theories of comedy have proliferated through the ages with almost as much regularity as theories of tragedy. Let the philosophers and the psychologists dispute; the great comic playwrights—Aristophanes, Shakespeare, Molière, Sheridan, Shaw—not only knew how to make their audiences laugh, but those of succeeding generations as well. The proof is in the survival of their plays. Human absurdity is no less a universal than human grandeur. Despite the fact that comedy is tied more directly than tragedy to the social fabric of the age, great comedy succeeds in transcending its specific social detail. Last week's Bob Hope monologue is already old hat, but *Lysistrata* will be contemporary as long as men fight wars, or women protest them.

The teacher of drama must, therefore, guard against the student's assumption—reinforced by untold hours of subjection to inane television situation comedy—that comedy is less "serious" than tragedy. In the hands of the great comic writers—and performers like Chaplin, we might add—comedy represents more than mere escapism. If the tragic writer expects us to participate in the power and the glory of human conflict, the comic writer invites us to watch man's entanglements with amused detachment. It is no less a vital task, for if man is capable of infinite heroism and suffering, he is also capable of infinite stupidity and absurdity. The comic writer warns us against taking ourselves too seriously. He does this in various ways: he can use the devices of satire (not, of course, confined to the dramatic genre) to measure not the norm but the ideal of human conduct. The more intense his awareness of the discrepancy between how men behave and how they are capable of behaving (as in Ben Jonson's *Volpone*, for example) the more bitter and bleak his comic vision. If the intensity of the contrast becomes so great as to make him lose his detachment, his work stands in danger of losing its comic balance.

Dramatic comedy moves on a scale between the extremes of "low" and "high" comedy; the worlds of farce and comedy of manners. Occasionally the comic modes are pure, but often we find several different modes combined, as the presence of farcical elements in the romantic comedy of *Twelfth Night* or in the high comedy of *The School for Scandal* demonstrates. High comedy usually presents the most difficulties for the student, for by its very nature it is based more on wit than on humor, and wit is less concerned with demonstrating human folly than with commenting upon it. Comedy of manners—as represented most purely in English drama of the Restoration—is, therefore, usually dependent upon a very specific set of social values. The laughter which it provokes has its roots in our sense of superiority to the foolish values and characters presented. Gaucherie, maladroitness, pretension—these are the salient vices of its world; cleverness, articulateness, savoir faire—these are the prescribed virtues. The Man of Mode is necessarily contrasted with Sir Fopling Flutter. To understand the world of high comedy, therefore, the student must have some awareness of the social values which underlie the play, for they may be quite different from his own. It is also necessary for him to be familiar with the historical context of the play if the humor is to be comprehensible, for high comedy is preeminently social comedy. It is for these reasons that high comedy is the most difficult of comic modes to perform well. The actors must have a thorough familiarity with the manner of behavior of the characters they are playing. American performances of English Restoration comedies are, therefore, almost always disasters. The figure of the fop, for example, is invariably played as an effeminate homosexual, which he definitely was not, as his hot, if foolish, pursuit of available females indicates. It takes companies steeped in traditions of theatrical finesse—like the French Comédie Française—to make high comedy succeed theatrically; traditions which, like good wines, do not travel well.

Needless to say, comedy of manners has never been a particularly American genre; our wit has always remained too egalitarian to accommodate the epigrams of a leisure class; we have no theatrical high comedy tradition. The American comic genius, represented perhaps more effectively in our films than in our plays, has been in the world of farce. It has been claimed by several critics that farce represents an inferior type of comic expression, that it bears relationship to comedy analogous to that of melodrama to tragedy. I do not share this view. I feel, rather, that farce presumes a specific set of comic conventions. All comedy to some extent exploits our enjoyment of the discomfiture of others. It permits us

to laugh at the misfortunes—psychic or physical—of comic characters with an openness our moral properties would inhibit in real
life. The *farceur* exploits comedy's freedom from moral restraint by
creating a world in which the real consequences of often disastrous
human conflicts are suspended. Duels, adultery, physical disabil-
ity: hardly laughing matters in the real world, but the raw material
of farce. The *reductio ad absurdum* of all conventions of farce may
be found in the sadistic animated cartoon in which characters are
repeatedly mutilated and annihilated only to be resurrected to
confront the next assault of their tormentors. Although good farce
is rarely so monomanically crude, it does demand that the audience acquiesce in the creation of a world in which the laws of
probability are willfully suspended or grossly exaggerated. Much
farce is indeed mere escapism, but it can be more than this. The
world the *farceur* creates—however caricatured—can often very effectively depict an intense view of human absurdity. "A mad world,
my masters!" This is the message of farce, as much of the work
of Aristophanes, Molière, Goldoni, Wilde—and Chaplin, Keaton,
and the Marx Brothers affirms.

TWO ANALYSES

Since my subject is an immense one, I have been necessarily
general in my treatment of it. Let us now apply several of these
generalities to two familiar plays in the hope of clarifying by specific example.

Death of a Salesman

Almost every critical discussion of Arthur Miller's *Death of a
Salesman* becomes enmeshed in the question of whether or not the
play is a tragedy. Miller himself partially invites this because of
his conscious striving for tragic universality; for example, his
naming of his protagonist Willy Loman (low man) deliberately
invokes comparison with the traditional "high man" whose down-

fall constitutes the subject of classic tragedy. But the question "Is *Death of a Salesman* a tragedy?" invariably produces more heat than light as critics become entangled in the larger and even more abstract question of whether or not contemporary tragedy is indeed possible. Ultimately, critical judgments seem to reduce themselves to the more basic question of whether *Death of a Salesman* is an effective and moving drama. If the critic thinks it is, he invariably claims tragic status for it; if he doesn't, he compares it invidiously with the great tragedies of the past.

I think we can see, therefore, that the *least* fruitful approach to the play—certainly for beginning students of drama—is to pursue the will-o'-the-wisp of tragic definition. Well, then, what meaningful questions can be asked? Essentially, the same questions we ask in confronting any work of art: what is the author getting at? What means does he use to communicate his concerns? How effectively does he communicate them? How significant are the concerns themselves? How imaginatively has he used the conventions of the particular genre in which he has chosen to work?

To apply what we have stated generally earlier: one effective entry into the play can be achieved by considering the playwright's use of theatrical convention. What is the theatrical style of *Death of a Salesman*? The individual scenes seem to be essentially illusionistic—the characters, for example, speak the language of everyday life—but listen to Miller's description of the setting:

> Before us is the Salesman's house. We are aware of towering, angular shapes behind it, surrounding it on all sides. . . . As more light appears, we see a solid vault of apartment houses around the small, fragile-seeming home. An air of the dream clings to the place, a dream rising out of reality. The kitchen at center seems actual enough, for there is a kitchen table with three chairs, and a refrigerator. But no other fixtures are seen. . . . The entire setting is wholly or, in some places, partially transparent. The roof-line of the house is one-dimensional; under and over it we see the apartment buildings. . . .

The setting, then, is *not* illusionistic. We are presented with the skeleton of a house through which we can see the oppressive "angular shapes" of the city. Miller indicates, moreover, that the actors do not always observe the imaginary wall lines, that in scenes of Willy's imaginings the characters can enter or leave a room by stepping "through" these "walls." As we continue to read the play we see that it often rejects the rigidities of naturalistic drama. Scenes from Willy's past and obsessional images like his brother Ben break the flow of the continuous present. Miller objectifies Willy's fantasies and reveries in charting his path toward self-destruction. And yet the play abounds in specific detail; the playwright never loses his grip on social reality.

What is the style of *Death of a Salesman* then? Although I am suspicious of labels—they are often convenient substitutes for thought—I think we might call it "selective illusionism." The characters do not acknowledge the presence of the audience, they are conceived within a specific social context, they function as recognizable, life-size human beings—but they are embodied in a play which does not attempt to present on stage a precise, imitative vision of reality. Clearly, Miller wants to have the best of both stylistic worlds: he wants the density of realistic detail because his drama is rooted in concrete social realities, but he does not want to be bound by the limitations of naturalism. His play does not remain fixed in one setting, and he does not want the scenic designer to be forced to provide completely illusionistic settings every time the scene changes. After the failure of his first Broadway play, the illusionistic *The Man Who Had All the Luck*, Miller wryly observed that the director spent so much time rehearsing the moving of scenery that he forgot to rehearse the actors.

From discussing the theatrical conventions of the play—which would be greatly aided by a photograph of the Mielziner setting —the teacher should move to the next important question: why did Miller use this particular style? Why, for example, did he not use a bare stage, as Wilder did in *Our Town?* On consideration it can be seen that a bare stage would not suit Miller's purpose, for he is not using the Loman family as the microcosm of all human experience, as Wilder attempts in chronicling the Webb and Gibbs families. It is important that Willy's house be dwarfed by the omnipresent towering apartment houses in performance, for like the elms in O'Neill's *Desire Under the Elms* they contribute to the claustrophobic mood essential to the play's theme. Willy is destroyed not by cosmic forces but by society; he is destroyed because he accepts values which contradict his real nature. Content in his garden, using his hands to build creatively, he nonetheless is convinced that success must inevitably fall to one who is "well liked." If there is tragedy in *Death of a Salesman,* it is social tragedy, and society should make its presence felt on stage.

Willy's disintegration represents the entire movement of the play. Insofar as "point of view" exists in drama as in fiction, in *Death of a Salesman* the point of view is entirely Willy's. We not only follow his every action these last two days of his life, but retreat with him into his past to discover the roots of his dreams, deceptions, anxieties. Miller wants us to understand Willy as thoroughly as possible, and therefore uses every device of his craft to explore Willy's character. We see Willy reliving his happy memories of simonizing his old car, playing ball with his kids, exulting in Biff's football triumph. We also see Willy brooding guiltily over his deception of Linda in Boston. We see Ben appear and reappear as a leitmotif—ethereal, unrealistic—the embodiment of the success Willy yearns for but can never achieve: "When I walked into the jungle, I was seventeen. When I walked out I was twenty-one. And, by God, I was rich!" Obviously, the devices of naturalism could not serve to render so inclusive a portrait.

And when Willy is briefly offstage, Miller takes the opportunity to drive home the significance of Willy's disintegration. In defending Willy to her sons—and indirectly to us—Linda states:

I don't say he's a great man. Willy Loman never made a lot of money. His name was never in the paper. He's not the finest character that ever lived. But he's a human being, and a terrible thing is happening to him. So attention must be paid. He's not to be allowed to fall into his grave like an old dog. Attention, attention must be finally paid to such a person (Act I).

The accusation has been made by unfriendly critics that the "attention" demanded by Linda is out of all proportion to the immediate situation, that Miller is trying to force the audience to accept Willy's downfall as more significant than it actually is. Whether or not we accept these judgments I think we must admit they raise pertinent questions—which might profitably be pursued in the classroom. Mary McCarthy, one of Miller's most hostile critics, has pointed out that "no one could write an editorial calling attention to the case of King Lear." Miller does indeed have a tendency to tell us how we should feel about Willy rather than allowing us to reach our own conclusions. He tends to make painfully overt what should be demonstrated through dramatic action. Again, Charlie at Willy's funeral asserts that "nobody dast blame this man. A salesman is got to dream, boy. It comes with the territory."

How damaging is Miller's tendency to universalize consciously? Does the play itself lead to the judgments of Linda and Charlie? It is my feeling that Miller *has* succeeded in establishing Willy's importance, both as a suffering individual and as a member of society. *Death of a Salesman* challenges certain basic assumptions of American society, and we falsify the play if we do not confront Miller's criticisms. Willy's downfall is meaningful in larger terms because he has accepted—according to Miller—false values which are nonetheless deeply rooted in American culture. What does Willy sell? We never learn because the product is unimportant. Willy is a salesman; his job is to sell a product—any product—regardless of its worth. And how does one sell a product? Not by its intrinsic value, but by the power of its advertising or the personality of its salesman. This is Willy's dream: like Dave Singleman, the old salesman, to sit in his hotel room and without leaving it pick up the phone and make his living. It is Miller's contention that it is a false dream: Willy drives hundreds of miles a day, dragging his heavy sample cases, only to meet indifference or scorn. Finally, in the name of business efficiency he is cast away "like a piece of fruit." But he holds his dream to the end. There is no recognition scene in *Death of a Salesman*. Willy's very suicide is based on the false assumption that his boys will finally use his insurance money to achieve the success he missed. Biff finally realizes this: "Charlie, the man didn't know who he was." But Happy will carry on Willy's false pursuit of success: "I'm not licked that easily. I'm staying right in this city and I'm gonna beat this racket!" (Requiem) *Death of a Salesman* is, therefore, a play which forces us to examine the basic values of ourselves and of our society. It should be the teacher's task to aid the student in this examination.

The School for Scandal

Sheridan's great comedy represents one of the hardiest survivors of the English comic tradition. Although it is tied very closely to its age, it nonetheless succeeds in exposing universal human absurdities; the "man of sense" may no longer exist as a specific social type, but moral hypocrisy has surely not disappeared. Nor was the age of gossip-mongers and scandal sheets purely a late eighteenth-century phenomenon. I do not think we should have any difficulty in finding contemporary equivalents of Lady Sneerwell, Mrs. Candour, and Sir Benjamin Backbite. Note the names: the teacher might well approach the play by asking his students why Sheridan chooses such overt, typical indicators of his characters' basic personalities. Why does he not merely reveal their traits through dramatic action rather than indicating them immediately through their names?

And so a word about high comedy—the comedy of manners—is

appropriate. The teacher can ask the student to compare the different kinds of comedy with which he is familiar in order to make important distinctions between comic modes. Some basic historical material should be introduced so that he is aware of the developing comic tradition. Indeed, to really appreciate *The School for Scandal* it is necessary for the student to recognize what Sheridan was reacting against and what he was affirming in the English comic tradition. Far from obscuring the play, this historical understanding, I believe, can contribute vastly to the student's appreciation of its universal comic elements. Judgments based on knowledge are always preferable to those based on ignorance.

The student should be made aware—to what extent depends upon his age and sophistication—of some of the basic trends of the comic tradition of the seventeenth and eighteenth centuries. Sheridan was very consciously trying to revive the spirit of Restoration comedy, which had been smothered by a century of sentimentality. Restoration comedy was aristocratic, urban comedy whose values were profoundly anti-middle-class. The rake, the seducer—if he operated within established codes—was viewed not as the villain, but as the hero in the comedies of Wycherley, Etheredge, and Congreve. The country wife and her cuckolded husband (as types represented by Sir Peter and Lady Teazle in *The School for Scandal*) were the objects of derision, as were the bourgeois virtues of fidelity and chastity. Needless to say, when the bourgeoisie came to power and established its values on the stage, it was shocked and dismayed by the "immorality" of aristocratic Restoration comedy. The ideal of the lighthearted love game was replaced by the sanctification of the institution of marriage, and the rake, no longer free to pursue his amoral designs through innumerable seductions, bowed down before the "man of sense," the embodiment of middle-class virtues. The new comedy was almost the antithesis of its predecessor and was dominated by an overly conscious morality. Indeed, this moral stance so succeeded in robbing comedy of both wit and humor that sometimes it is difficult for the reader to distinguish between sentimental tragedy and comedy, so similar are they in mood and style.

Inevitably this ponderous comedy of moral platitudes and "poetic justice" brought forth its detractors in the persons of Oliver Goldsmith and Richard Sheridan. Sheridan wanted to rid comedy of the solemnity which was burying it and looked to the example of Restoration comedy. But while Sheridan decried sentimentalism, he was—as a man of his time—inevitably influenced by it, and we do not find in either *The School for Scandal* or *The Rivals,* his two great plays, the identical amoral Restoration vision. To compare *The School for Scandal* with, say, *The Country Wife* or *The Way of the World* is to be aware of profound differences in theme and comic device which belie the plays' superficial similarities. Despite the satiric attack on Joseph Surface, the hypocritical "man of sense," Sheridan does not counter with the values of Horner or Mirabell (the heroes of the former plays). He ends *The School for Scandal* with a device dear to the heart of sentimental drama: the reformation of "wicked" characters. Indeed, Charles hardly needs reforming. He is "wicked" on the surface alone, as his name indicates. Despite his profligate spending and drinking, he is good-natured, honest, and generous—indeed, sentimental as his attachment to the portrait of Sir Oliver indicates—at heart a good fellow merely sowing his wild oats. Similarly, Lady Teazle comes to realize that Sir Peter is not a doddering old cuckold (compare Mr. and Mrs. Pinchwife in *The Country Wife*), but a good, honest, reliable husband. How Wycherley and Congreve would have hooted at Sheridan's dénouement!

Sheridan is, then, very much of his age. Although structurally and thematically he returns to the world of Restoration comedy (for the most part he avoids bourgeois characters), the benevolent rationalism of sentimental comedy is still felt in his work. But in Sheridan's masterful hands this sentimentalism is used to good advantage. Despite the satiric attack on hypocrisy and scandalmongering, there is a geniality and good nature in Sheridan's plays to which we immediately respond. The hard brittleness of Restoration comedy is softened, as Sheridan never falls into the excessive bitterness which often diminishes the comic effects of the plays of Wycherley, for example. Indeed, for all his emphasis upon the witty aspects of high comedy—as in the scenes of *The School for Scandal* in session—Sheridan is also successful in reviving—perhaps for the first time since Ben Jonson—genuine comic humor. The reader, and certainly the viewer, of *The School for Scandal* instantaneously recognizes Sheridan's skill in exploiting comic situations. Both Restoration comedy and the comedy of sentiment had, for all their essential dissimilarity, one point of contact: both lacked the humor which arises from comic situation or character; in the case of the former, the demands of wit predominated, and in the case of the latter, moral principles were forever paramount. There is nothing in all of Restoration or early eighteenth-century comedy to compare with the incomparable screen scene (Act IV, Scene 3) of *The School for Scandal*. Sheridan does not hesitate to use the devices of farce to create one of the most brilliantly drawn scenes in all of dramatic literature. Moreover, Sheridan possessed a keen sense of plot. Unlike the Restoration comedies of wit, and in particular the comedies of Congreve, *The School for Scandal* is never bogged down in such a multiplicity of plot entanglements as to render their recollection well-nigh impossible. Sheridan returns to the methods of the Elizabethans in that in his play there is no dichotomy between the comic situation and the comedy itself. Because of this, *The School for Scandal* remains the most accessible of all English comedies of manners. Above all, it is immensely actable, as anyone who has seen it in performance can attest.

By clarifying these historical considerations, the teacher is able to remove the barriers between the student and Sheridan's comic genius. Once he is no longer puzzled by the very real linguistic, social, and theatrical difficulties which the play presents, the student can easily respond enthusiastically to its wit and humor. With the ground cleared, the teacher can concentrate on demonstrating Sheridan's masterful comic technique, perhaps by a close reading of the screen scene: the way the playwright skillfully builds to Charles' disclosure of the hidden Lady Teazle, and his and Sir Peter's wonderfully contrasting exclamations: "Lady Teazle, by all that's wonderful!" "Lady Teazle, by all that's damnable!" The greatness of the scene lies in the fact that its farcical elements are directly related to character development. Joseph Surface's hypocritical machinations are his undoing, and Sheridan exploits our joy at his discomfiture, for Joseph represents a type he thoroughly dislikes. But Sheridan, as his satirical attack on the slanderous "school" indicates, is never malicious. Lady Sneerwell asserts that "there's no possibility of being witty without a little ill nature. The malice of a good thing is the barb that makes it stick." But Sheridan's point of view and comic approach are surely reflected in Sir Peter's rejoinder: "Ah, madam, true wit is more nearly allied to good nature than your ladyship is aware of."

6

On Teaching Essays

DON L. COOK

Associate Professor of English,
Indiana University

One of the most attractive qualities of the essay is its humility. It is, after all, only a try. Other genres, tragedy and romance for instance, are spoiled if their formulae are not fulfilled. A tragedy that is deficient in its catharsis of pity and fear is no tragedy at all. Because it sets for itself such exalted goals, because it takes itself so seriously, tragedy presumes genius. But a mere man may write an essay. Even the novel, whose form is protean and whose aims and effects are enormously diverse, often awes us with the complexity and depth of its meanings. Given the kind of analysis that George Levine provides elsewhere in this volume, *Great Expectations* turns out to have an intricacy and integration of parts that daunt our attempts to embrace all of its multiple meanings. Modern psychology and an appreciation of ambiguity and unconscious revelation only remove us further from a feeling of human fraternity with the creator of a masterpiece of fiction. While Dickens and Melville, Shakespeare and O'Neill stretch our consciousness of the range of human experience, the adult reader, and how much more the responsive adolescent, is sometimes more astonished than delighted. The brilliance of the new atmosphere and the new company is so dazzling that the senses resist. No man can know that much, can manipulate words with that complex precision, can reveal to us so much of ourselves.

And yet, a mere man may write an essay. In so remarking I do not, of course, mean to deprecate the essay nor to elevate drama and fiction unduly. But in any discussion of teaching literature I think it is important to consider both the availability of the literature to the students and the nature of the response that we can reasonably hope to elicit from those who will respond at all. For a teacher who hopes to take students beyond passive acceptance of literature and into an active and analytical appreciation of it, one of the greatest initial roadblocks is the students' tacit assumption of the inevitability of a work of art. Why is it written this way? Why does Chillingworth emerge from the forest to find Hester standing on the scaffold? Why is it again in the forest that Hester and Dimmesdale plan their escape? Why is Billy Budd afflicted with a stoppage of speech? Why should it be in a chapel-like bower of trees that Henry Fleming finds a corpse whose eyes suggest the side of a dead fish, and why should he, a moment earlier, have noticed a small animal pounce upon and capture a gleaming fish? The initial response is likely to be, "Because that's the way it happened." While that response is soon shown to be inadequate, the mental set on which it rests is not so easily routed. The great initial attraction of fiction, its illusion of life, is also its most stubborn block to analysis.

If analysis of prose fiction is obstructed by the tacit assumption that it is essentially a transcription of an action, the opposite mental set has to be overcome when we teach poetry. Clearly poetry is not the mere transcription of an experience. It is stylized; indeed, students tend to demand even more stylization than many poets are willing to provide. The heavier the rhythm and rhyme, the further the poetry is from ordinary speech, the more secure the students feel in regarding a work as genuine poetry. But if poetry is not life it is surely open to the suspicion that it is the product of mystical inspiration. The beauty of poetry is likely to be interpreted as the product of a finer-than-mortal nature. Keats and Shelley and Wordsworth transformed their worlds into poetry, but they were, after all, Keats and Shelley and Wordsworth. The young reader is more apt to picture them rapt in contemplation of a beatific vision than besieged by alternative verbs or competing images. It is difficult for students to believe that Shelley sweat or that Wordsworth threw down his pen. But even students know that essays are not inspiration; they are prose, just words. A successful essay says a thing clearly and memorably. It is required to do no more. An essayist does not have to be inspired as does a poet; he does not have to encompass mankind as does a novelist. He only has to have a thing to say, and even that may be only tentative.

The views I have presented here are of course vastly simplified. But students or even adults who have not thought much about literature tend to hold simplistic views. One often notices a kind of resistance or even resentment against any attempt to analyze literature. The tacit assumption is that the pleasures of literature are emotional, not intellectual, that art speaks to the heart, not to the mind. That proposition is not entirely without truth, but in full flowering, it leads to the "I don't know much about ——, but I know what I like" syndrome. It is precisely in connection with this attitude that the humility of the essay can be of great service to the teacher of literature.

The essay does speak to the mind. The best essays don't stop there, but the mind is the initial, obvious target of the essayist. If he is inspired, it is not with a fine frenzy but with a fine clarity. If he encompasses the multiplicity of human experience, it is for the purpose of examining, ordering, and clarifying it for his reader. Ambiguity and paradox are not necessarily beyond him, but his aim is not merely to register them as part of human experience but to comment upon them, to try their variety and clarify their significance. He is not exempt from wonder, but his responsibility is to say what he thinks about the source or the fact of his wonder.

The essayist's position is relatively exposed. He has not the novelist's devices of character, setting, and action to distract attention from his own presence. Nor has he the poet's incantation as a protective screen. However artistic and polished his performance, the essayist is essentially an individual thinking aloud. And the act of thinking aloud led Montaigne to give the genre its name to begin with.

The French verb *essayer* contains a multitude of hints of the attractions of the essay: to try, to try on, to attempt, to make a trial of, to assay, to try one's skill, to try one another. Each of these is within the scope of the essay. When Montaigne began to compose little *leçons morales,* rather than merely to collect them from his reading, he called them *Essais.* He thus indicated that these were his attempts to come to grips with a subject, tentative tries at formulating his observations and meditations. Both Montaigne and his ideas were on trial before their audience. Bacon, too, consciously chose to assay ideas rather than to plead for them. He speaks of two kinds of prose, one "magistral" and the other "probative." The magistral voice, he said, is designed to persuade an audience, but of course the writer who employs that voice must operate from "a ground of certitude." The probative style, which he employed in his essays, is better suited to the exploration of ideas. The writer in this case proposes rather than preaches. He offers not final truths, but hypotheses. He sets up his ideas as challenges to the minds of his readers. This is not to say that he abandons his skill in rhetoric. An idea deserves the best setting it can be given, and what clarity, balance, antithesis, parallelism, economy, and wit can do for an idea, Bacon does. It is not merely the originality of the idea, but the skill of the statement that arrests us in such Baconian aphorisms as: "Suspicions amongst thoughts are like bats among birds, they ever fly by twilight" or "As the baggage is to an army, so is riches to virtue. It cannot be spared or left behind, but it hindereth the march."

This aphoristic style is perhaps Bacon's greatest contribution to

English letters. Its charm for the reader is obvious; it is witty, close-packed, striking, and memorable. It is the encapsulation of an atti-tude. To the author, too, its appeal is great. It is personal; it rests on no historical, logical, or legal argument but rather on the per-spicacity of the aphorist. While he may want to illustrate his point in order to render it clearer, he need not prove it. The force of his personality, acting through an acute rhetoric, is the aphorist's chief resource. The aphorist aims not to bring his reader around to his view by the slow accretion of evidence but to startle him into recognition and acceptance of the aphorist's "truth." For this reason the most interesting and lasting essays have often been those that reveal unconventional points of view toward ordinary experience. When William Hazlitt tells us, "No young man be-lieves he shall ever die," or when Emerson says, "Let us treat the men and women well; treat them as if they were real; perhaps they are," we are struck not by their logic or learning but by their origi-nality and force of mind, by their wit. We believe or accept not because we are argued into submission but because the essayists have confronted us with their personal formulations and have tacitly challenged us to propose better.

THE BENEFITS OF THE ESSAY

It seems to me that there are three benefits available to the student of the essay. The first, aesthetic pleasure, is not radically different from that available in fiction and drama, but it is perhaps more pure, that is, less complicated. There is for instance less escape in it, less tendency to lose oneself in the writer's experience and to empathize with his sensations and emotions. Like any gen-eralization, this is a dangerous oversimplification. Surely essays like George Orwell's "Shooting an Elephant" or "A Hanging" in-volve us deeply in the progression of events and even more deeply in Orwell's emotional responses to them. But even in these essays the narrative interest and emotional involvement serve a more abstract end. Finally we are most interested in what Orwell *makes* of his experience, what ideas he abstracts from it. It is his very skill at abstracting the meaning from his experience that militates against his chances of being remembered as a first-class novelist. Too often his novels strike the reader as being illustrations of ideas rather than compelling experiences. The movement of his mind is vastly more interesting than the lives of his characters. Seldom has a great novelist been a great aphorist or vice versa. One cannot, I think, imagine E. M. Forster writing, "every white man's life in the East, was one long struggle not to be laughed at." And yet how perfectly this aphorism of Orwell's harmonizes with the felt experience that *Passage to India* provides us.

The esthetic pleasure of the essay then tends to be abstract, to inhere in the words of the writer, in the juxtaposition of ideas in his mind. The essayist is above all the manipulator of semantic symbols. At one end of the scale is the pleasure we feel in allow-ing S. J. Perelman or James Thurber or Robert Benchley to tickle our minds with unexpected turns of idea or phrase. Into this cate-gory falls Benchley's remark, "I don't know why I should feel that I am immune from trial by a jury of my peers—if such exist." The sudden and witty revelation of the movement of the author's mind is a source of minor delight. But the recognition of man thinking may be a shock as well as a delight, and indeed in our own day much of the confrontation of deep realities, once ritually expressed through tragedy, has been assumed by the essay. In his superb essay, "Many Thousands Gone," James Baldwin allows us a fas-cinating glimpse of a mind at work. "Time," he says, "has made some changes in the Negro face. Nothing has succeeded in making it exactly like our own, though the general desire seems to be to make it blank if one cannot make it white." His play on "white" and "blank," his temporary assumption of a white persona through which to speak, the wit that crackles the surface of his deep seri-ousness: all of these contribute to the power of his ideas and at the same time attract us to the mind from which they flow. The essay is personal not because it is autobiographical, but because we are convinced that we have been in touch with the personality behind the page.

It seems to me that this is what the essay has to offer as an initial attraction for the student. Like the novel's illusion of real life, this contact with the working mind of an author, though not the end of the process, is a powerful attraction on which the teacher can build. The mental excitement and restlessness with which many students respond to such old-hat writers as Emerson and Thoreau is proof that students are amenable to this appeal. The very brevity of the essay often enables them to concentrate their normally fragmented attention long enough to be moved or shaken or delighted. This esthetic shock of recognition and communication is then the first benefit I claim for the essay.

Once a student's attention is arrested by Thoreau's statement, "We do not ride on the railroad; it rides upon us," he is ripe for an inquiry about why the statement arrested him. There is no character identification to cut through. The student can see immediately that he has been affected by an arrangement of words, by a structure of semantic symbols. There was nothing inevitable about their choice or arrangement, though certainly linguistic conventions, the same ones that govern each student's writing, bounded Thoreau's practice. A student can't really be expected to imagine what David Copperfield would have been like had Dickens made Miss Murdstone a generous and sympathetic character. Even in short stories, hypothetical revisions change the meaning so radically that there does indeed seem to be something almost inevitable, something beyond human device, in the creation of fiction. But the essay is less sacrosanct, more malleable. One can readily experiment with a different combination of Thoreau's words or may select totally different words with which to try to express his idea. One can keep the meaning in mind and try various expressions of it. Not only is the mind of the author the source of the student's esthetic pleasure, it is the stimulus rather than the suppressant of his critical perception.

A student who has responded to style and has begun to be aware of the conscious artistry, by which his response has been controlled has taken a long step toward the development of conscious style in his own writing. I am sure that we have all had the experience of reading the work of a striking stylist for an extended period and then finding, when we began to talk or to write, that the rhythms and patterns of the stylist lingered in our ears and strove to impose themselves upon our thoughts. The old-fashioned idea of learning to write by imitation has many things to recommend it, not the least of which is that we do so whether we intend to or not. But critical examination of style, an examination facilitated by the humility of the essay, is essential if the student's writing is to be under his control. Otherwise imitation may become unconscious parody as do the pretend telephone conversations of toddlers who make the sounds but are irresponsibly unconscious of the meanings they convey.

The relative ease with which a student may be brought to a critical stance vis-à-vis the essay brings us to the third benefit I promised, creative impetus. Because the student can respond rather directly to the words and mental processes of the author, because he can discern the operation of the style, he is closer, in the essay, to the creative experience than he is likely to be in any other genre. In his discussion of the teaching of poetry, Philip Appleman wisely suggests that attempts to write poetry are a valuable adjunct to its study. The same thing is true of the essay, and, in addition, how much nearer to a satisfying product the students are likely to come if their aim is a polished aphorism, an incisive paragraph, or even a controlled and stylistically consistent brief essay. Probably the greatest inducement to effort and experiment among adolescents is the possibility of success in a more adult role. The smart-aleck remarks we hear from them are really trial flights at sophisticated repartee. The same urge to demonstrate independent judgment and individual distinction can be tapped by a teacher who shows students that the essay is at once adult and demanding, and yet available to them as an arena in which to test their ideas and personae. It provides for them an opportunity to experiment with both words and roles and yet does not demand that they declare any overtly literary intentions. They, like Montaigne, are only essaying ideas, only testing the strength and suppleness of their minds and styles.

TEACHING THE ESSAY

In teaching the essay, as in teaching any other genre, analysis is an indispensable tool. The same caution, of course, applies to the essay as to other genres: don't analyze the life out of the literature, and don't let the analysis become an end in itself. But just as mere palpitation is an inadequate response to poetry or mere identification a debilitating response to fiction, mere acceptance or rejection of the thesis leaves a good essay unsavored and unsounded. The fact that the essay is nonfiction is liable to lead students to think that the quality of an essay can be decided by the percentage of the audience that is ready to assent to its proposition on first reading. In fact, if the teacher permits the discussion of any essay to begin with a judgment on its merit, the session is likely to deteriorate into a debate over the students' reactions to the thesis, or worse yet, into a debate on the validity of the beliefs which have preconditioned the students' reactions.

It is essential, of course, that students understand the major point of the essay, and that preferably at the beginning of the discussion. But this can be managed by careful assignment of and preparation for the essay. While one is naturally reluctant to kill the impact of an essay by paraphrasing it before the students have read it, a teacher can safely set the essay in the context of the author's general views, or in the context of literature already discussed. One can define key terms on which the essay turns and either assign or suggest questions which will direct students to central rather than peripheral issues. I frequently ask students to select a sentence which best sums up the author's point or, if they find none to satisfy them, to write such a sentence, as far as possible in the author's words. Other questions will vary according to the qualities and opportunities of the essay and the aims in teaching a particular essay. I think it is very dangerous to assign lists of words to be looked up and questions about grammatical or syntatic features. Only words that are essential to a grasp of the major ideas should be assigned. Others may need discussion in class, but excessive drudgery, though it may build the student's vocabulary until the end of the week, may permanently demolish his enjoyment of reading. Matters of grammar and syntax are best examined in terms of the intentions and choices of the author, not merely to illustrate what loose and periodic sentences are or to demonstrate the ways in which independent clauses may be legally joined. For one thing, modern essayists are dangerous authorities to appeal to for support on grammatical rules. Some of the most interesting contemporary essayists, such as Kazin, Baldwin, Kempton, McDonald, Ellison, Hoffer, and Eisley, are as likely to undercut a prescriptive ruling as to support it. Besides, the essay, if we are going to bother to teach it as essay, is not just reading assigned to build vocabulary and promote familiarity with the conventions of language. If the student is asked to observe the author's use of conjunctions, or lack of conjunctions, the student should expect to find that the author had been artful in their use or disuse. There is not much point in directing attention to those aspects of an author's writing that are entirely conventional unless he achieves some extraordinary ends by ordinary means.

After the student has read the essay and completed the assigned questions, one of several tactics may be fruitful in the classroom. Consideration of a single word or a single sentence will often focus the attention of students on the conscious workmanship of the writer. The class can then work toward an exploration of the author's ideas, but the base for the exploration is not a generalized emotional response but specific words selected and manipulated by the craftsman. The writer's choice of words leads directly to his choice of sentence structure and of tone. These in turn raise questions of the relation he has sought to establish with his audience and of the tactics by which he has tried to influence the response of that audience. If we can get this far in objectifying the piece of writing, it is unlikely that the discussion will slip back into the familiar "I don't like it where he says ———." Attention is focused on the problem the writer set for himself and on the resources of tactic, tone, vocabulary, and syntax he employed in the solution of that problem. Ultimately, evalution must take place, and the reader's personal experience and beliefs cannot be excluded from such evaluation. But if the analysis of the writing has been successful, the students should be ready to make their evaluations in terms of the writer's skill rather than of the harmony of his thesis with their own emotional predispositions.

Perhaps a paragraph from Emerson's "Self-Reliance" will illustrate the point:

> For nonconformity the world whips you with its displeasure. And therefore a man must know how to estimate a sour face. The by-standers look askance on him in the public street or in the friend's parlor. If this aversion had its origin in contempt and resistance like his own he might well go home with a sad countenance; but the sour faces of the multitude, like their sweet faces, have no deep cause, but are put on and off as the wind blows and a newspaper directs. Yet is the discontent of the multitude more formidable than that of the senate and the college. It is easy enough for a firm man who knows the world to brook the rage of the cultivated classes. Their rage is decorous and prudent, for they are timid, as being very vulnerable themselves. But when to their feminine rage the indignation of the people is added, when the ignorant and

the poor are aroused, when the unintelligent brute force that lies at the bottom of society is made to growl and mow, it needs the habit of magnanimity and religion to treat it godlike as a trifle of no concernment.

The discussion might begin with attention to the word "feminine" in the last sentence. Why *feminine*? How does this word link with *decorous* and *prudent* and with *senate* and *college*? Why are the "cultivated classes" "vulnerable themselves"? ·Which words does Emerson use in the last sentence to emphasize the difference between the displeasure of the cultured and that of the uncultured? Does the diction successfully convey his contention that one is more dangerous than the other? With which group does he deal in the more abstract terms? Earlier he speaks of "sour faces" and "sweet faces" and of "a sad countenance." Which term implies the most genuine emotion? Is Emerson's phrase "as the wind blows and a newspaper directs" merely repetition and amplification of one idea or does the phrase convey two ideas? The paragraph consists of eight sentences; they are, in order, 8, 12, 15, 51, 17, 20, 15, and 57 words long. Does their length conform to the movement of Emerson's ideas? Which one or ones carry his greatest concentration of idea? In the last clause of his last sentence Emerson uses the term *godlike*. To what kind of behavior does he apply this term? How does the term harmonize with the title of his essay? Does his advocacy of "the habit of magnanimity and *religion*" conflict in any way with his advocacy of self-reliance? How does this paragraph prepare the reader for Emerson's later question, "have [we] not lost by refinement some energy, by a Christianity, entrenched in establishments and forms, some vigor of wild virtue? For every Stoic was a Stoic; but in Christendom where is the Christian?"

Obviously not every paragraph of an essay the length of "Self-Reliance" can be examined in this detail, but there is merit in demonstrating and having the students practice fully alert reading. If it seems that I am violating my own warning about avoiding analysis as an end in itself, let me suggest that after a close reading of even three or four paragraphs of "Self-Reliance" the students will be able to discuss Emerson's ideas a great deal more cogently and with a decreased tendency to accept or reject them on the basis of emotional predilection.

Some essays unfold best if we begin at the other end and examine the writer's general tactics before we turn to word choice. George Orwell's "Shooting an Elephant," for instance, contains few of the obscurities for students that Emerson's sometimes dated locutions impose. And too, Orwell's diction is much less continuously abstract. Eleven of the fourteen paragraphs are narrative, and while close examination is not wasted upon them, neither do they require the kind of explication Emerson's paragraphs deserve. Orwell's essay makes a much tidier point than does Emerson's. "Shooting an Elephant" is briefer, more obviously structured, and, for an American teenager, less subjectively controversial. These are points that the students might be brought to discover in their study of the two essays, but, more crucially, they are facts which dictate a different plan of approach for the teacher.

The point that Orwell makes is not terribly complex, and students are likely to be able to find or to compose a fairly adequate thesis statement before the discussion begins. Attention then can be quickly turned to the question of how Orwell makes his audience, most of whom have had no experience of British or any other colonialism, *feel* the rightness of his thesis. What is it on the one hand that permits Emerson to argue in the abstract, to rely on metaphor and simile and analogy to clarify and enforce his points, but on the other hand causes Orwell to devote eleven of his fourteen paragraphs to a first-person narration of the execution of an animal? Is it just Orwell's whim? Is it just Emerson's dearth of experience? Or is it that, in the final analysis, the idea of colonialism is inherently more abstract than the idea of self-reliance? Could Orwell depend upon his audience to have the experience upon which a personal response to his thesis could be based?

While his essay is lengthy and complex, and some of his terms dated, Emerson is still talking about the interior experience of self-doubt, about timidity masquerading as modesty, about the intimation of undeveloped personal excellence that we have all felt, though we may never have put words to our feelings. Emerson hits close to the reader's response to "Self-Reliance" when he says, "In every work of genius we recognize our own rejected thoughts; they come back to us with a certain alienated majesty." Much of Emerson's power derives from his ability to say memorably what his reader already feels. He can be abstract because the concrete basis for his abstraction is already within his reader.

Orwell can't. If Orwell is to achieve anything more than a polite assent to the proposition that colonialism was a degrading business—a proposition which no civilized reader is likely either to dispute or to feel much exercised about—then he has to provide the reader with the concrete experience that gives force to the abstraction. And the whole point of our discussion is to find out how he pulls off that trick.

What is the function, early in the essay, of Orwell's statement, "I thought that the greatest joy in the world would be to drive a bayonet into a Buddhist priest's guts"? Does not this admission, coupled with his admitted hatred of empire, help the reader to empathize with Orwell's plight and prepare the reader to undergo the shooting with the same ignobly mixed feelings to which Orwell confesses? Is not Orwell building a bond of humane feeling and human inadequacy between himself and the reader? How does Orwell's treatment of the two corpses "work" in the essay? The first is the Coringhee coolie, whom he discovers "lying on his belly with arms crucified and head sharply twisted to one side. His face was coated with mud, the eyes wide open, the teeth bared and grinning with an expression of unendurable agony." But he quickly breaks into the description, with parenthesis no less, to say, "(Never tell me, by the way, that the dead look peaceful. Most of the corpses I have seen looked devilish.)" He interrupts his narrative, and his dramatic scene, to speak directly to the reader in colloquial and even callous terms (*Never tell me, most of the corpses, devilish*). He consciously disassociates his sympathies, and the reader's, from the coolie who has fallen prey to the rampaging elephant, a natural though dangerous force. But when he allows himself to be bullied into shooting the elephant, largely to avoid looking a fool before the natives he has been sent out to govern and to enlighten, he gives the reader a movingly detailed account of this pointless, degrading, and avoidable slaughter. Never are we allowed to look away. Not once does Orwell relieve the tension by a callous or even disinterested remark. We are made to go through the agonizing moments with Orwell, to watch the elephant "beating his bunch of grass against his knees, with that preoccupied grandmotherly air that elephants have." We look through the telescopic sight with Orwell as he pulls the trigger and observes that, "in too short a time, one would have thought, even for the bullet to get there, a mysterious, terrible change had come over the elephant. . . . He looked suddenly stricken, shrunken, immensely old. . . ." Then for over five hundred words we and Orwell watch the elephant live on in its torture, "breathing very rhythmically with long, rattling gasps . . . dying very slowly and in great agony, but in some world remote from me where not even a bullet could damage him further." Orwell says, "In the end I could not stand it any longer" and we agree. This second death is the one that indicts the colonial system and the one that Orwell must make us experience if we are to acquire a concrete basis for understanding his abstract thesis.

But Orwell does not, of course, forgo all further responsibility, as a short story writer might legitimately do. In a final paragraph he comments upon the experience he has given us. Employing irony with a skill worthy of Swift, he quotes his fellow officer's remark that "an elephant was worth more than any damn Coringhee coolie." One suspects him of commenting on his own technique as a writer at the same time that he reinforces the thesis he has built.

This kind of analysis does not, I think, destroy esthetic pleasure. If we help the student to conceive of the essay in the terms Montaigne proposed, that is, as a trial flight of an idea and of a mind, then much of the pleasure will derive from seeing the idea stay aloft. What keeps it aloft? What prevents its descending into banality, dullness, or obscurity? What powers its flight and gives it buoyancy? These are the questions that arouse and engage the critical perception. And finally as he comes to recognize the techniques and devices of the writer and to experience the vicarious pleasure of watching ideas hatched, fledged, and launched forth, a student may be moved to try his own powers of creation. He may never write a poem. He may lack the imagination required for the creation of fiction. But the humbler urge, to try an idea, may prove to be the creative impetus he needs.

7

On Teaching Biography

C. DONALD PEET

Associate Professor of English,
Indiana University

Biography at present seems much less highly regarded by teachers and critics of literature than fiction, drama, or poetry. Although thousands of copies of biographies are sold every week to readers of all kinds, the craft of biography itself receives singularly little attention in literary circles. The men who keep us supplied with more books and articles than we can find time to read on the theories and techniques of poetry, drama, and fiction tend for the most part to ignore biography. They have nothing to say against it, but they simply do not discuss it. When a new biography from some prominent specialist in this genre is published, its author will very likely be invited to write a short essay for *The Saturday Review* or *The New York Times Book Review* in which he discusses his problems and purposes. But the book itself will probably be reviewed by a historian instead of a literary critic, unless it happens to be about a writer, and its merits or defects will probably never become the subject for an analytical essay by any of the men who dedicate themselves primarily to the study of literature. They will continue to concentrate on poems, plays, and novels; and if they meet a young writer whose talents merit encouragement, they are much more likely to urge him to write a poem, play, or novel than a biography.

THE STRENGTH OF BIOGRAPHY

To explain the literary critics' lack of interest in biography by defining it as a form of history rather than of literature is to raise the general question of the relative merits of these two disciplines. The classic statement of the inferiority of history to imaginative literature may be found in Sir Philip Sidney's famous *Apology for Poetry*. Sidney defined poetry so broadly that nearly all the arguments he raised in its defense can be used on behalf of novels and plays as well. Its chief function, he maintained, was to serve as an instrument of moral instruction. Poetry provided men with striking examples of virtue and vice in action. It presented these examples in so pleasing a way that men would study them gladly and amend their lives accordingly. While histories are also filled with examples of human actions, good or bad, they are inferior to works of imaginative literature in elevating the moral stature of their readers. As Sidney saw it, the historian's duty of recording events exactly as they had happened, without being able to modify them for the sake of enforcing some valuable lesson, necessarily prevented him from matching the poet in didactic effectiveness. Indeed, "the historian, being captive to the truth of a foolish world, is many times a terror from well doing and an encouragement to unbridled wickedness." His commitment to factual truth obliges him to record all too many instances of virtue unrewarded and vice triumphant.

No one today is likely to use Sidney's argument to maintain the superiority of fiction, in verse or prose, to that kind of historical writing we call biography. No one is likely to defend any of the liberal arts in the moralistic terms that came so naturally to men of the past. Didactic theories of literature and history have long been out of fashion. But if modern literary critics do not expect writers to compose moral *exempla,* they still wish works of imaginative literature to display what they call a "meaningful insight

into life," or a "significant ordering of experience," or something of
that sort. They do not look for moral lessons, but they do demand
faithful and thought-provoking representations of the complexity
of existence as we know it.

It would seem that a writer could provide such representations
by writing history as well as fiction, or biography as well as drama.
But something similar to Sidney's belief in the inferiority of historical works to fictional narratives prevails in literary circles
today, quite possibly because of the basic distinction which Sidney
emphasized. A historian or biographer cannot exercise the kind of
control over his material that a playwright or novelist can. His
plot has been determined for him in advance. He is tied to facts
which he cannot alter to present his own vision of life. One could
even argue that the more a biographer imposes order on the dis-
organized events of his subject's life, and the more selectively he
emphasizes or passes over events in that life to develop his own
view of the nature of things, the more of an artist he becomes—
but the less of a biographer.

Yet the biographer's function as a recorder of actuality, even if
it prevents him from exercising the kind of control over his material that a playwright or novelist enjoys, is his strength as well as
his burden. More than thirty years before Sidney wrote his *Apology*, a claim for the superiority of history to fiction had been vigor-
ously stated by the French bishop Jacques Amyot in the preface
to his translation of Plutarch's *Lives*. Amyot had defended history
with substantially the same arguments Sidney was later to use for
imaginative literature. History gives men examples of wise or
foolish conduct, and examples affect men more strongly than do
abstract ethical precepts. They teach men "how to choose in
doubtful and dangerous cases" that which may be for their own
profit: and can show an individual "how to moderate himself in
prosperity and how to cheer up and bear himself in adversity."
(I quote from Sir Thomas North's translation, first published in
1579.) But whereas Sidney proceeded from this point to claim the

superiority of fictional to factual examples, Amyot had advanced precisely the opposite view. For him, history or biography "doth things with greater weight and gravity than the inventions and devices of the poets; because it helpeth not itself with any other thing than with the plain truth, whereas poetry doth commonly enrich things by commending them above the stars and their deserving." Because biographers like Plutarch tell us "the plain truth," what they say must command our attention or respect in a way denied to any fictional narratives. Even if the events they describe seem improbable, artificial, or contrary to normal human experience, we cannot dismiss them as we would the unconvincing incidents in a play or novel unless we can show that these events have not been recorded accurately. Otherwise, we must stretch our ideas of what is possible or probable so that they will fit the facts with which biographers confront us. We must come to terms with the "plain truth."

The sophisticated modern historian may very well be amused at Amyot's confidence in the biographer's ability to tell us this "plain truth" about what happened in the past. He may also be embarrassed by Amyot's flat assertion that history or biography is "a certain rule and instruction which by examples past teacheth us to judge of things present and to come." Few men can speak with such certainty today about the value of history or any other discipline. Still, if the ordinary high school or college student is asked what possible benefit he may gain from his history courses, he will probably answer with Amyot's ideas, if not his words. The student's teacher may prefer a more subtle and less hackneyed defense of history, but his students will persist in seeing the past as primarily a guide to the present and future. Likewise, the student who prefers reading a biography to a novel—and we know that a good many do—will defend his preference by arguing the superiority of fact to fiction. Novelists can make anything they like happen in their stories; biographers have to tell the real truth.

Naïve though this view may be, it does recognize the distinctive strength of biography, and the teacher who challenges it does so at some risk. He may quite properly point out the difficulties a biographer faces in discovering the precise details of any event, much less the causes and effects of that event. He may observe that just as the plot of a novel reflects and implies the novelist's personal view of life, so a biographer's selection of events to emphasize in his subject's career necessarily depends upon his subjective evaluation of what is or is not important in a man's existence. He may show that biographies and novels both invite us to contemplate events which their authors find significant. He may argue that the difference between the imaginary happenings of a novel and the actual events of a biography means little to an experienced reader who can find the same kind of satisfaction or stimulation with either kind of book. But to the young reader, the credibility of biography as opposed to the fantasy of fiction will remain its most distinctive and valuable feature. The prudent teacher will make the most of this faith in the truthfulness of biography, rather than fight it.

If biography's most distinctive quality as a literary genre is its fidelity to truth, and if this quality is its most important characteristic in the eyes of the student, then whatever approach to biography a teacher chooses to take in his classes should always involve some consideration of how biographers gather accurate information, how this information may be presented in different kinds of biographies, and what signs or symptoms of inaccuracy an astute reader will keep alert for. Just as a conscientious biographer will never grow so infatuated with the techniques of narrative fiction that he neglects his obligation to factual accuracy, so the capable teacher of literature will never let his enthusiasm for artistry in biography lead him to underestimate its importance as a true record of what actually happened somewhere at some time, a valid sample of human experience. Without entirely neglecting the ways in which a biographer's work resembles that of a novelist or playwright, he will encourage his students to respect a biographer's accomplishments in narrative technique—the degree of skill he displays in organizing or dramatizing his material—chiefly insofar as it contributes to a full and faithful realization of the biographer's subject. Whether we define biography as primarily a literary or a historical genre, and whether we agree with Sidney or Amyot concerning the relative merits of history and literature, we must still recognize that the strength of biography is the strength of truth. The primary characteristic of the teacher as well as of the writer of biography must therefore be a respect for truth.

SOME VARIETIES OF BIOGRAPHY

There are many ways, however, in which the truth may be told. Although the high school English teacher can hardly be asked to devote class time to a detailed consideration of all the possible varieties of biography, he can be reasonably expected to make his students aware that biographies can be written in a number of different ways, all of which have their advantages and disadvantages, and all of which can be quite successful if handled with sufficient skill and dedication to the strength of truth. We may discriminate among these different kinds of biography in terms of the extent to which their authors interpose themselves, as guides, interpreters, or instructors, between their subjects and their readers.

The presence of the author is least obvious in what can be called the *documentary biography,* the story of a man's life presented entirely or almost entirely through the documents in which the evidence of his existence is recorded—legal records, church registers, personal letters, newspaper items, and the like. The authors of such biographies are responsible for the selection, arrangement, and annotation of the documents they publish; they do not, however, attempt to interpret these documents or to weave them into a sustained narration. Among the best examples of this form are the documentary biographies of Schubert, Handel, and

Mozart by Otto Erich Deutsch, the distinguished German musicologist. Students of literature may be more familiar with Jay Leyda's *The Melville Log* or Leyda's later attempt to employ this method on a more recalcitrant subject in his *Years and Hours of Emily Dickinson.* Sir Edmund Chambers' *William Shakespeare: A Study of Facts and Problems* (published in 1930 but still considered the most authoritative single source of information on Shakespeare's life) is basically a collection of all the available documents on Shakespeare with an extremely elaborate and painstaking commentary on them. Documentary biographies may be as bulky as Chambers' two large volumes or as short as the many "casebooks" on particular persons or events, like the Sacco and Vanzetti trial or the battle of Gettysburg, which have been published in great numbers during the past ten years or so, chiefly for use in college composition classes. These little books provide the simplest way, as I will explain later, in which the study of documentary biography can be introduced into high school, as well as college, classes.

All such books are essentially collections of raw material which has not been processed by its compiler into a biographical narrative of the more usual sort. The merits of such a book depend sometimes on its author's skill in unearthing significant documents but always on his judgment in selecting the most important of whatever documents may be available for inclusion in his volume. The accuracy with which he transcribes these documents for his readers is also a major consideration, since making absolutely accurate copies of old documents, whether printed or handwritten, is a much more tedious and demanding task than may be supposed by those who have never tried it. Beyond this, the value of documentary biographies depends on the supplementary matter supplied by their compilers to make it possible for readers to evaluate the documents intelligently. Forgotten incidents or obscure references in the documents must be explained; the context of excerpted passages from longer documents must be indicated; sometimes the precise reason for the inclusion of a given document must be made explicit. Although the documentary biographer is committed to the idea of letting his facts speak for themselves, he must sometimes supply more than a few footnotes to make these facts speak loudly and clearly enough.

Even so, such a biographer for the most part keeps himself concealed behind his documents. The extent to which he organizes or explains his materials for his readers' benefit may be so slight that his book may not appear to be a true biography at all. It leaves what is perhaps the most difficult part of a biographer's work—synthesizing the evidence at his disposal—entirely to the reader. While this distinctive characteristic of the documentary biography makes it an extremely useful textbook for any teacher who wishes his students to gain experience in thinking things out for themselves, it normally produces a book which no ordinary student can be expected to read with profit unless he receives considerable help.

Of the more conventional kinds of biography, what we usually think of as a *scholarly biography* comes closest to the collection of documents in its degree of authorial objectivity but at the same time offers a coherent narrative of its subject's life. The scholarly biographer normally produces a chronological record of his subject's career in as much detail as his facts permit, making his dependence on documentary evidence entirely clear and never venturing far from what the documents tell him. Books of this sort usually offer a maximum of factual information concerning their subjects, but a minimum of theorizing on the implications of this information. Scholarly biographers, like the compilers of documents, present the evidence upon which someone else might base a psychological analysis, moral evaluation, or personality portrait of the men who are their subjects; but as a rule they refrain from such speculative undertakings.

Of the many biographies of this type, Leslie Marchand's three-volume study of Lord Byron's life is especially noteworthy for its thoroughness and readability. The documentary evidence for the facts of Byron's life is so abundant that for some periods an almost day-by-day (or at least a week-by-week) account of his doings is possible. This is the sort of narrative Professor Marchand provides. He builds his biography out of all the factual evidence which Byron's earlier biographers had discovered and out of the data which he himself found in the course of his research. He does not scorn to include even what seems to be the most trivial sort of information: the measurements recorded by Byron's tailor at various times in his life, for instance, or the details of the diets which Byron frequently employed to keep his weight down. On remarkably few occasions, however, in the course of his three volumes does Marchand permit himself to generalize on all the data he presents. He tells us in great detail what Byron did and offers cautious opinions on Byron's thoughts, feelings, and motives, insofar as they can be determined; but he does not try to "explain" Byron, to trace a pattern in his life, to dig beneath the surface of his mind in search of the psychological roots of his actions, or even to describe in detail Byron's achievements as poet.

When reviewing Marchand's biography for *The New Yorker*, shortly after its publication, W. H. Auden was particularly interested in the facts about Byron's weight and shape provided by the records of his tailor. Noting how much weight Byron gained during relatively short periods of time and how drastically he was forced to diet at intervals throughout his life, Auden came to the conclusion that Byron must have suffered from a hypothyroid condition or something of that sort. Plausible as this suggestion may be, it is the sort of conclusion which a scholarly biographer like Professor Marchand would hesitate to draw, even if he were privately convinced of it. While even the most cautious scholarly biographer is forced to indulge in some speculation from time to time, he avoids it as much as possible and always keeps his readers aware of the difference between fact and theory. His tendency to interpret the facts at his disposal as conservatively as he can will disappoint

any reader who is looking for a full evaluation of the subject's life.
But the reader who likes to draw his own conclusions will be
grateful for the great body of information with which he has been
provided and will accept this information with all the more confidence in its reliability because its compiler displays so scrupulous
a regard for demonstrable facts.

Most readers, however, including students at all grade levels,
prefer biographies in which the discernible facts of the subject's life
are not so much recorded as dramatized. Biographical facts can be
dramatized only if the biographer permits himseilf considerable
freedom to enrich his narration of these facts with his own significance. The dramatic realization of any happening requires more
detail than documentary evidence ordinarily provides. The imagination of the biographer supplies this needed detail in what we
may call the *popular biography*. The author of such a biography
is partly a historian but also partly a novelist or dramatist. He does
not try to list as many facts about his subject as he can; rather, he
selects only what he regards as the most significant facts and interprets them as fully and freely as he sees fit. His chief intention
is not to discover new information about his subject; instead, he
draws heavily upon the work of his more scholarly predecessors
and concentrates on organizing or interpreting the knowledge he
gains to what he considers its best advantage. To avoid interrupt-
ing the flow of his narrative, he seldom makes his readers aware
of disputed points in the history of his subject or of the precise
reasons why he chooses to follow one version of a given incident
rather than another; to the contrary, he usually narrates the events
of his story as if there were no doubt as to what happened to
whom at what time and for what reason. He takes what the
scholarly biographer would call probabilities—perhaps even possibilities—and treats them as certainties.

To draw these contrasts between scholarly biographies and
those in the more popular vein (including the works of such well-
known writers as Lytton Strachey, Emil Ludwig, Hesketh Pear-

son, Catherine Drinker Bowen, and Marchette Chute), is not necessarily to deny the value of these popular biographies. While many of them cannot be taken seriously by either the historian or the literary critic, a respectable minority are well written, carefully planned, and intelligently executed. Perhaps the greatest advantage such biographies enjoy over the more scholarly sort is that they are not intended only for those readers who already are interested in their subjects. No one is likely to start reading a large scholarly biography unless he already has a strong interest in its hero—or unless he is a student who has been sentenced to write a term paper. But popular biographies are designed to attract that hypothetical being, the general reader; and their success may be measured by the frequency of their appearance on the best-seller lists. They are planned to stimulate the reader's interest as well as to satisfy it. Even the reader of scholarly tastes can find much to value in the best of these books. For him, as well as for less demanding readers, they make admirable introductions to personalities or events which he can investigate more carefully afterward, if he wishes. For the ordinary student, such books are invaluable in enlarging his knowledge of the past and his understanding of the many ways in which life may be lived.

Popular biographies, like novels or plays, are usually organized to develop some theme or controlling idea which reflects whatever value the biographer sees in recording the life of his subject. Some biographers value their subjects largely as representatives of their times, their callings, their social classes, or their particular philosophies of life. They may write on Marlowe as the characteristic man of the Renaissance, Rembrandt as the archetypal artist, Napoleon as the self-made man, or even Beau Brummel as the dandy of dandies. Some biographers are psychologists at heart and seek the underlying motives and desires which governed their subjects' careers in the hope of enriching our understanding of the mysteries of the mind. All too frequently biographies are written to substantiate the biographer's personal philosophy of life. A

few, ordinarily addressed to younger readers, are deliberately designed to inculcate lessons in morality—or expediency. But most
of the popular biographies which come from the press today seem
to be written mainly for the sake of whatever dramatic, exotic, or
romantic situations they enable the biographer to recount for that
considerable number of readers who look for little more.

In this respect, they do not differ from most novels and plays.
Popular biographies resemble works of imaginative literature also
with respect to many of the narrative devices their authors usually
adopt. We can tolerate and perhaps enjoy the popular biographer's use of such devices so long as they do not lead him into
gross distortions of the truth—although as teachers, we are obliged
to make our students aware of their artificiality. We need not
necessarily object to his putting speeches into the mouths of his
characters, so long as these speeches are derived from (or at least
do not contradict) the reliable documents on which any legitimate
biography must rest. Turning the usual indirect discourse of historical records ("he said that he was innocent") into direct discourse for the sake of dramatic immediacy ("he said, 'I am innocent!'") need do no serious damage to truth if handled with
discretion. Likewise, the popular biographer's usual assumption
of the ability to read his subject's mind—to tell us exactly what he
was thinking when he did this or said that—need not be con-
demned. The mature reader may prefer books with a minimum of
such more or less fictitious additions to the factual record, but
will not automatically reject books which contain them. He will
probably base his judgment on whether the biographer's imaginative additions to his factual material seem to clarify or to
confuse the significance of this material.

The fundamental requirement for accuracy in all biographies,
however, can never be entirely relaxed, even when we are reading
books which their authors call *biographical novels* or *nonfiction
novels*. (I am indebted to Irving Stone for the first phrase and to
Truman Capote for the second.) Even though such books may be

called novels by their writers, they are normally read as biographies by their readers. The success of such books with the general public depends as much on their reliability as witnesses to what men actually said and did as on their authors' skill in writing dialogue or composing vivid descriptions. The authors of these books are fully aware of this. Thus we have Irving Stone appending several pages of acknowledgments and an extensive bibliography to his "biographical novel" on Michelangelo, *The Agony and the Ecstasy*, and Truman Capote insisting that his "nonfiction novel" *In Cold Blood* is as faithful to fact in every respect as he could possibly make it. These authors know that if their books of this kind were presented to us primarily as works of fiction, our reaction to them would necessarily change. Although *In Cold Blood* is not a biography in the usual sense of the word, it deserves attention here because it illustrates so well the main advantage that a book of fact has over a book of fiction. It purports to give us the precise facts of a singularly ugly crime and to acquaint us in some depth with the men responsible for this crime. If the crime or the criminals were only the product of Capote's imagination, we could read *In Cold Blood* as we read any novel, accepting or rejecting the view of life it implies according to our own standards of judgment. But if Capote's narrative is a true and complete record of the men and events with which it deals, then we cannot reject it simply because it fails to satisfy our personal expectations of reality. Instead of criticizing the book, we must change our habits of thought. We must enlarge our view of life to fit the facts with which we have been presented.

The power to make this demand upon readers is the supreme strength of any biographical or historical narrative. Even in the "nonfiction novel" or the "biographical novel," the price which must be paid to gain this strength is fidelity to fact. Thus the truthfulness of all the kinds of biographies we have considered must be a major concern to us when we read or teach them. The only books of a biographical or historical nature in which the accuracy of an author's portrayal of men and events is a matter of minor significance are those we call *historical novels*. These books combine a substantial quantity of obviously fictitious matter with a more or less accurate depiction of bygone times and important men and women of those times. If we were to demand from them the same degree of factual reliability we look for even in popular biographies, we should find ourselves obliged to reject many a novel or play which generations of discriminating readers have valued highly. Shakespeare's history plays, for instance, contain frequent and deliberate deviations from the facts recorded in the history books that Shakespeare used. But works of historical fiction, plays or novels, may be distinguished from those forms of biography which can never sacrifice truth with impunity because of the different expectations which we, as readers, bring to them. The amount of pure fiction found in such works makes it clear that they are not to be read primarily as historical records. We are under no compulsion to regard the contents of these works as hard facts of human experience.

This is not to say that we cannot, if we wish, read such books mainly for the history they can teach us. I once had a friend with a passion for seamanship who read C. S. Forester's splendid Hornblower tales largely for what they could teach him about British ships and naval practices in the days of Lord Nelson. But most of us are relatively indifferent to the truth or falsity of historical novels. We do not care whether Tolstoy's description of the battle of Borodino is reliable in all respects or whether Thomas Mann really knew how Egyptians thought and talked in the days when Joseph the Hebrew became chief steward to Pharaoh. We judge historical novels as we judge all novels, with regard to their plots, their characters, and the ideas embodied in these plots and characters. In view of the historical novel's relative freedom from the requirements of factual accuracy, the fact that so many popular books of this type are actually more distinguished as history than as fiction is truly ironic.

ESTIMATING THE RELIABILITY
OF BIOGRAPHIES

We may agree that all biographies, whatever their nature, must be judged largely in terms of their fidelity to Amyot's ideal of the "plain truth," but when we read a book about someone of whom we have little or no prior knowledge, how can we estimate its reliability? If we are teachers, how can we decide which biographies deserve to be recommended to our students or adopted as texts for classroom analysis?

Unless we grow extremely interested in a particular book, we are hardly likely to find time for any detailed investigation of the accuracy of its statements; and if we find the time, we may not have the facilities we need for such inquiry. We can and should, of course, consult the opinions of the presumed experts who review the book for responsible journals. The prompt and readily available reviews in such publications as *The Saturday Review* and *The New York Times Book Review* may provide us with the kind of criticism we need. But such reviews are often too short and sketchy, if not too hastily prepared, to enjoy much authority. More informative reviews of scholarly biographies can be found in the academic quarterlies, but popular biographies of the sort we are most often concerned with are usually ignored by such journals. In any case, none of us likes to abdicate altogether his own responsibility of decision to some reviewer, no matter how distinguished the reviewer's credentials may be. Can we not somehow draw upon our own resources as careful readers to form at least a tentative estimate of a biography's credibility?

I think we can. There are no professional secrets I can reveal to transform us all into unerring judges of biographical accuracy, but there are a number of common-sense considerations which are worth keeping in mind whenever we evaluate biographies. The problem is essentially one of judging the author's character as it is revealed in what he writes. Any writer can make mistakes. We want to know whether the writer of the book before us is especially prone to err because he lacks sufficient respect for the facts he presents or because he lacks the judgment to interpret these facts properly. Any writer will exhibit his individual beliefs, attitudes, or feelings to some degree in his works. We want to be on guard against the writer who consciously or unconsciously distorts his subject in the interest of his own predilections. There are many ways in which a biographer can unintentionally betray his unreliability, but perhaps the most obvious are *inconsistencies* between the events he narrates and the conclusions he draws from these events, and *inadequate or illogical explanations* of the causes of these events.

The brief character sketch of General Grant included in the third book of Vernon L. Parrington's *Main Currents in American Thought* provides a striking example of biographical inconsistency. According to Parrington, Grant was "short, stooped, lumpish in mind and body, unintellectual and unimaginative, devoid of ideas and with no tongue to express the incoherent emotions that surged dully in his heart." Harsh though this description may be, Parrington could conceivably persuade us of its truth by presenting incidents in Grant's life to substantiate it. What he does, however, in his very next paragraph is to review Grant's career in such a way as to destroy his own summary of Grant's shortcomings. He tells us that while Grant served in the Mexican War, he regarded it as "a stupid imperialistic debauch" and that not long afterward, "oppressed by the eventless routine of garrison life, he fell into the habit of solitary drinking." Something is wrong here. Does a soldier who is "devoid of ideas" look on a war in which he is serving as an "imperialistic debauch"? Does a man who is "lumpish in mind" and "unimaginative" grow so oppressed with dull routine that he seeks an escape in alcohol?

With sufficient ingenuity we may be able to think of some way in which these apparent contradictions can be reconciled; but

Parrington does not help us. He seems quite unaware of how his account of Grant's life contradicts his picture of Grant's personality. The prudent reader, however, sees inconsistencies of this sort as unmistakable evidence of carelessness, to say the least, and estimates Parrington's reliability accordingly. If he happens to know that some military historians have called Grant's campaign to capture Vicksburg the most imaginative of the entire Civil War, he will have further cause to doubt the truth of Parrington's description; but he need only read the pages before him with careful attention to the implications of each sentence to realize that something must be wrong.

Few biographers, of course, can be trapped in such obvious inconsistencies. A more typical example of how a biographer may entangle himself in partial or outright contradictions may be found in W. J. Turner's much admired *Mozart: The Man and His Works*. In his seventeenth chapter, Turner describes Mozart's music as possessing a "flawless perfection" unmatched in the works of other composers; whether we look at one of Mozart's most significant or most casual works, "we are confronted with a completely finished musical composition in which there is not a superfluous bar, not a redundant or meaningless note." Turner seems to have forgotten that in his sixteenth chapter he made a point of Mozart's having had "striking and significant second thoughts" about quite a number of his works and having revised them to their great improvement. Turner cannot quite have it both ways. If none but perfect pages came from Mozart's pen, how could he or anyone else improve them by revision? If Mozart's taste were so refined that all his works display "flawless perfection," why should he have had "second thoughts" about any of them, signifying his dissatisfaction? Turner's inconsistency could, of course, be corrected by minor changes in his statements involving the substitution of more restrained terms than those he employs. Even so, this single instance of inconsistency is enough to warn the astute reader that Turner's rhetoric (or simply his love of Mozart's music) may run away with him at times; and such a reader will stay on guard against any more serious violations of logic or disregard for, facts.

The errors of Turner and Parrington are typical of those into which biographers may fall when they greatly admire or severely deplore the subjects of whom they write. Their strong opinions lead them to exaggerate; their exaggerations produce inconsistencies.

In some ways, however, occasional inconsistencies in a biography are more easily forgiven than insufficient or illogical explanations. Too often, especially in popular biographies or "biographical novels," a writer confronts us with some unusual facts about his subject's character or actions and then either fails to suggest any cause for these facts or else offers one which is patently inadequate. In either case his failure to provide a plausible explanation for the facts he narrates raises doubts as to the plausibility of these facts themselves. In *The Agony and the Ecstasy*, for example, Irving Stone emphasizes Michelangelo's compelling desire to carve or paint men and women in the nude. He shows us Michelangelo expressing this wish as a boy of thirteen or so and makes it clear that in this respect Michelangelo was in sharp conflict with the prevailing artistic practice of his time. We may naturally wonder why so young a boy should hold so unconventional an opinion and should champion it so strongly, in defiance of his elders. Stone, however, offers no explanation for Michelangelo's desire. He asks us, in effect, to accept it as a fact for which no reasons can or need be given; and it may very well be a fact, for all I know. Nevertheless, if a novelist were to endow his main character with so unusual an attitude, to emphasize the unconventionality and the importance of this attitude, and yet to provide no motivation for it, he would be inviting his readers' incredulity.

A biographer cannot flout plausibility with impunity any more than a novelist can. He may, of course, confess his inability to discover exactly why his subject thought and acted as he did (though a "biographical novelist" like Stone can hardly make such a confession). But whenever he raises questions in his reader's mind—questions such as why did Michelangelo want to depict the human body unclothed, where did he find the self-confidence to defy his teachers, patrons, or critics, and why, when well past puberty, did he pay no attention to girls—and then leaves these questions unanswered, he cannot complain if his reader begins to grow suspicious of his knowledge or judgment. Perhaps the chief weakness of *The Agony and the Ecstasy* is its author's consistent inability to explain how or why Michelangelo became the man and the artist in whom he wishes us to believe.

From Vasari's sixteenth-century biography of Michelangelo, Stone learned that the artist had been suckled by the wife of a stone-cutter. Stone incorporates this fact into his narrative apparently to justify his belief that even as a boy Michelangelo was determined to become a sculptor rather than a painter. Very likely Stone realized how odd such an explanation would seem to most modern readers, for unlike Vasari he also lays stress on Michelangelo's having spent much time watching stonecutters work and helping them a little during four of his childhood years. If he had been content to explain his hero's early preference for sculpture only by referring to the occupation of the husband of his wet nurse, he would have given us a striking example of an explanation which must surely offend any adult reader's sense of logic.

Illogical explanations are usually the result of oversimplification. They are most frequently found, as one would expect, in biographies intended for younger readers. I am thinking now of books which imply that Lincoln became president because he read as much as he could in his youth or that Liszt became a great pianist because he practiced very hard. We expect and indeed require a certain amount of simplification in books for children; but there is a line beyond which simplification becomes deception. Even Benjamin Franklin comes close to this danger in writing his memoirs so that young people may learn "the effects of prudent and imprudent conduct in the commencement of a life of business." Franklin never actually says that hard work and a careful eye on the cash box were responsible for his achievements in the world, but too many readers have carried away that impression from his *Autobiography*. We may never be able to explain exactly what makes possible a career so remarkable as Franklin's, but if there is anything we can be sure of, it is that working a fifty-hour week and staying out of debt may keep a man off the welfare rolls but will never make him another Franklin.

Oversimplified accounts of causes and effects are not, however, found only in books intended for children and adolescents. Among biographies aimed at a mature audience, they are usually found in those books which concentrate on the psychological roots of their subjects' behavior. There is nothing inherently improper in a biographer's attempt to pick out the one or two events in his subject's early life which seem to have exerted the greatest influence on his future actions; there is no necessary harm in a biographer's use of psychoanalytic theories to suggest reasons for his subject's beliefs and endeavors. But when a biographer argues that the whole course of Henry James' life and the nature of his novels are the results of an injury of uncertain nature which kept him out of the Civil War; or when another biographer maintains that Joseph Conrad lived and wrote throughout his life under the sway of a guilt complex when he left his homeland as an adolescent; or when a third biographer tells us that Nietzsche's philosophy of the will to power was the result of his having grown up as the only male in a household of women, there is no reason why we should regard their explanations with more respect than we ordinarily show to those more characteristic of children's books, in which we read, for example, that Bach went blind in his sixties because as a little boy he had copied music by moonlight.

Any of these attempts to determine the cause-and-effect patterns in a man's life could be sound; but the reader who realizes how hard it is to determine the precise motives for the behavior of even the men and women he knows best will be slow to acknowledge any biographer's ability to explain so much with so little. Every biographer naturally looks for the critical moments in his subject's life. But if he combines a proper respect for accuracy with a mature awareness of the complexity of life, he will hesitate to ascribe too many effects to a single cause. He will be as sensitive to the dangers of oversimplification as he is to the risk of leaving important matters unexplained or to the peril of drawing conclusions which are inconsistent with the facts he has recorded. He will keep his book as free as possible from those symptoms of haste, carelessness, poor judgment, or prejudice to which we, as critical readers, will always be alert.

BIOGRAPHY IN THE HIGH SCHOOL

The deficiencies of any single biography do not diminish the value of biography itself. The difficulty we encounter in finding biographies which do not have shortcomings of one kind or another does not prove that biographies by their nature are untrustworthy guides to human experience and that they are thus less suitable for an English teacher's purposes than novels or plays. On the contrary, some study of the biographer's art, with particular attention to the ways in which he shares the responsibilities of the novelist or playwright as well as to his special responsibility of factual accuracy, seems highly appropriate to any plan of study designed to show students how literary works of all kinds reflect and criticize life as their authors know it.

In many schools at present, biographies are more often the subjects of book reports and term papers than of class discussions. Knowing that many of his students will choose biographies to satisfy out-of-class reading assignments, a teacher will naturally do what he can to see that the school library keeps an adequate supply of good biographies available for them—including a few of the documentary type for the benefit of those exceptional students who like to work things out for themselves and wrestle with the facts of the subject's life instead of having these facts pre-digested for them. In deciding which biographies he can recommend with the most enthusiasm to his students, the teacher may wish to keep in mind the considerations which have been discussed in this essay, and he may find or make opportunities to call these considerations to his students' attention, if only in the course of a class discussion about some biographical sketch of the sort usually found in textbook anthologies.

Likewise, the teacher who requires his students to present oral or written book reports will have frequent opportunities to illuminate the problems of biography in general by the suggestions he makes when students are preparing reports on biographical narratives and by the questions he asks when these reports are delivered or handed in. By asking his students how the biographer whose book they have been reading came to possess the knowledge he displays, and by inquiring as to the evidence this biographer cites to substantiate his conclusions, the teacher may stimulate students to ask the same kind of questions themselves in their future reading. He will have taken an important step toward producing readers who actively analyze the implications of what they read instead of passively absorbing whatever they find on the page before them.

Biographies lend themselves extremely well to assignments which require the writing of papers more demanding than ordinary book reports. If a student is especially interested in some famous man of the past, he may find the preparation of an extended paper in which he compares two or three different biographies of this man a less dreary project than composing a "research" paper of the usual sort. While most of the "casebooks" which publishers have been turning out for the past ten years or so are designed mainly for freshman composition classes in college, many of them are by no means too complicated or sophisticated for the use of high school students, and they provide plenty of material for written work, as well as for class discussion. If a teacher has reasonable freedom in choosing textbooks for his classes, he may wish to adopt one of these documentary texts as required reading for a unit of several weeks' duration, allowing plenty of class time for critical analysis of the book's contents and making one long or several short theme assignments which require the evaluation and synthesis of these contents. Most of these casebooks are short and easy to read. All of them, to one degree or another, challenge the student to become a biographer or historian himself, even if on a small scale. The value of such work is so obvious that a teacher who cannot make use of any published casebook may think it worthwhile to construct one of his own, using whatever resources his school library can supply.

A typical biographical casebook (or "sourcebook" as its publisher calls it), perhaps better suited for high school students than most, is *Julius Caesar in Shakespeare, Shaw, and the Ancients*, edited by G. B. Harrison and published in 1960 by Harcourt, Brace, and World. This book contains the full texts of Shakespeare's *Julius Caesar* and Shaw's *Caesar and Cleopatra*, along with Plutarch's biographies of Caesar, Brutus, and Antony, and selections from the writings of other ancient historians, including Caesar himself. It thus provides us with an opportunity to compare several different biographical accounts of Caesar with each other and with the interpretations of his character by two playwrights who gained their impressions of the man in part from these historical sources. The utility of such comparisons in illuminating the problems a biographer must solve and in clarifying the difference between the obligations of a biographer and those of a playwright is immediately apparent. Without necessarily using this particular book, a teacher could still obtain benefits of a similar nature by having his students compare Plutarch's Caesar with Shakespeare's or Shaw's or with the Caesar described by some modern historian (perhaps Will Durant in his *Caesar and Christ*) or with the Caesar of some relatively recent historical novel, such as Thornton Wilder's *The Ides of March*. He should have no trouble finding many different estimates of Caesar's character and accomplishments in the works of different historians. No matter how briefly or thoroughly he engages his students in analyzing and comparing differing accounts of this remarkable man, he should have little difficulty incorporating such a unit of study into any course in which Shakespeare's *Julius Caesar* is normally read.

Of course, no program of study calling for the analysis and comparison of varied biographical materials can be successful unless the teacher masters these materials himself before he turns his students loose on them. He is well advised, therefore, to choose some subject with which he already has a more than routine familiarity, as well as one which can be connected in one way or another with some of the literary works his students are reading or have read in previous years. Perhaps this is why Marchette Chute's *Shakespeare of London* is required reading in some high school English classes today.

Few English teachers can have acquired their degrees and certificates without having been acquainted to some extent with the facts of Shakespeare's life and times; and few students can go very far in high school without having been exposed to some of Shakespeare's more famous plays. But *Shakespeare of London* is so good a biography that even if teachers and students were less prepared to study the playwright's life than they are, this book could still be highly recommended for their attention. It is so clearly written that most students, except slow learners, can be expected to read and understand it without being led along chapter by chapter in class sessions. Careless readers may miss the point of some of Miss Chute's observations, but even they should be able to follow the main lines of her attempt to reconstruct Shakespeare's personal life and literary career. Thus a teacher could ask his students to read this book on their own time, perhaps to supplement the study of one of Shakespeare's plays in class, without anticipating any singularly bad results.

If I were using this book in a class of high school juniors or seniors, however, I should certainly want to spend at least a few class periods explaining how such books are written, how far the limits of their reliability extend, and what the specific merits and weaknesses of this book are. In doing so, I would be enlarging my students' knowledge of Shakespeare and at the same time increasing their understanding of biographical and historical writing in general. In addition, I would be trying, as always, to increase their awareness of the need for precision and sound logic in drawing conclusions from factual evidence. The benefits to be gained from studying so carefully prepared a biography are, in fact, so numerous that I might decide to spend more than a few days on it. The abundance and relative availability of books on Shakespeare and his times would make it easy for me to bring supplementary material to my students' attention, or to assign them to write papers comparing Miss Chute's views with those of other writers. If I did decide to spend two or three weeks on this book, exactly what features of it should I emphasize to help realize my general aims?

First, I should want to make my students aware of how a biographer today can learn enough about someone who lived hundreds of years ago to tell the story of his life. Since no one who knew Shakespeare personally ever wrote a biography of him, the modern scholar has no direct, first-hand testimony to the facts of Shakespeare's life. He must *deduce* these facts from whatever other kinds of evidence are available. Miss Chute's book is extremely useful for demonstrating the dependence of biographers on whatever documentary evidence they can find because she regularly makes quite clear the ultimate sources of her information on Shakespeare. Even though she does not footnote her text, as the author of a more scholarly biography would do, she usually mentions the specific documents she has used to learn the facts she records. I should make certain my students paid attention to her mention of these documents, whether they were church registers, depositions in a lawsuit, lists of plays and receipts in Henslowe's records, entries in the Stationers' Register, or the expense accounts of the Master of the Revels. Transcriptions and photographic reproductions of many of these documents may be found in *The Shakespeare Documents* by B. Roland Lewis (Stanford, 1940-41) and in many other books about Shakespeare's life and times certain to be found in any large library. The teacher with such books at his disposal can show his students just what such documents look like and how they read in their original form, so that the care and judgment a biographer must exercise will be evident.

Second, I should also emphasize how Miss Chute uses the technique of comparison to illuminate her subject. The comparisons she draws throughout her book between the Shakespeare family and the Quineys, their Stratford neighbors, as well as those between Shakespeare himself and some of his fellow playwrights in London, obviously help us to determine what was normal and what was unusual about the family and the man we are concerned with. Perhaps even more important, however, are the comparisons she makes between the documents on which our knowledge of Shakespeare rests and similar documents of the same period. Such comparisons are essential for the correct interpretation of any items of evidence which originated in a time or place remote from our own. Shakespeare's dedication of *Venus and Adonis* to the Earl of Southampton, for instance, has been misread by some biographers as a painful specimen of fulsome flattery, which shows that Shakespeare could be quite unscrupulous in seeking the favor of a powerful lord; others have mistakenly supposed that this strong affirmation of respect for the Earl necessarily indicates a significant personal relationship between the two men. Miss Chute, however, does not attempt to evaluate this dedication in isolation. She wisely reads it in the context of its time. By comparing it with the dedications written by other writers of the day, she is able to see that Shakespeare's dedication is neither exceptionally lavish in flattery nor especially personal in tone; and she quotes sufficient excerpts from some of these other dedications so that her readers may verify her opinion. The extremely messy condition of Shakespeare's last will and testament can also lead to dubious theories, unless this will is compared with others. Some biographers have tried to draw conclusions about Shakespeare's health or state of mind from the many deletions and interlinear additions found in this document. Miss Chute instead points out that Shakespeare's lawyer "was not in the habit of always making a fair copy of the wills he drew for his clients . . . and the nine-page will he made for John Combe, two years earlier, is also full of deletions and corrections." Thanks to her comparisons, she avoids another possibility of error.

Although *Shakespeare of London* is a popular biography, it is not a "biographical novel," and so its author can afford to confess ignorance about those parts of Shakespeare's life which are completely undocumented, such as the period between 1584, when his children Hamnet and Judith were conceived, and 1592, when Robert Greene alluded to him as an actor turned playwright. Her honesty should not pass without appreciative comment in the classroom. Likewise, she is not ashamed to say "probably" or "possibly" when the evidence for her views does not warrant a stronger degree of certainty. She rightly presents her theory that Shakespeare's wife did not accompany her husband to London because of her religious beliefs entirely as a hypothesis: "If Anne Hathaway had been brought up as a Puritan . . . . If Anne Shakespeare was a Puritan . . . ." Although her descriptions of the theatres in which Shakespeare's plays were first produced seem exceptionally complete, careful reading shows that she again declines to go beyond the limits of her evidence. She is aware that in spite of all the models of the Globe Theatre which have been built in schoolrooms throughout the English-speaking world, no one really knows exactly what it looked like or how Shakespeare and his fellow actors used it. Because she is not writing for an audience of scholars, however, she does allow herself to make plausible deductions from the documentary evidence without repeatedly warning the reader that her statements cannot be wholly verified. Our evidence for establishing the order in which Shakespeare wrote his plays, for example, or for determining the precise relationships between the reliable and unreliable editions of his plays published during his lifetime is insufficient to justify all the assurance with which Miss Chute handles these matters. It would be a good idea for a teacher analyzing this book in class to have some of his students find out just what evidence there is for the date when *Romeo and Juliet* or *Hamlet* was first performed, or to present such evidence himself and invite his class to consider its strength.

Although the merits of *Shakespeare of London* are so numerous and conspicuous that a teacher might feel an understandable reluctance to emphasize its possible flaws, an important aim of any detailed exploration of this book in the classroom should be to demonstrate that there are limits to the authority of even a good biography. Without descending to quibbling, a teacher can show that at times Miss Chute cannot be followed with complete confidence, either because she has neglected to investigate certain matters fully enough or because her opinions seem to rest on a doubtful estimate of probabilities. He can adopt the former alternative, of course, only if he happens to be well informed himself on some of the subjects with which this book deals.

A teacher who is familiar with the education provided by Elizabethan grammar schools could, for instance, show that Miss Chute's account of their deficiencies in her first chapter may be needlessly harsh. When she writes that "apart from teaching him Latin, Stratford grammar school taught Shakespeare nothing at all," she is not only overlooking the incidental benefits that six or eight years of studying a difficult language could offer a bright boy, but she is also neglecting the extremely elaborate training in composition and rhetoric which was an essential part of the Elizabethan grammar school curriculum. In those days boys were drilled in techniques of oral and written expression with a thoroughness we nowhere approach in our schools today. While much of this training may have been quite mechanical, it can be shown to have exerted a considerable influence upon Shakespeare's own style as a writer. By presenting more detailed information than Miss Chute provides on exactly what happened in Elizabethan classrooms, a teacher could help his students see for themselves that Shakespeare's school years were not altogether such a waste of time as Miss Chute suggests; and they could judge for themselves the degree to which her treatment of this stage in his life is misleading.

The teacher whose own training and interest do not permit him to challenge *Shakespeare of London* at any point in this way can at least read the book with a critical eye in search of places where its author's opinions appear to rest on questionable arguments. Unless he is more perceptive than I, he will find no unmistakable examples of the kinds of errors which we have previously considered—conclusions which are inconsistent with the facts on which they rest, or patently inadequate explanations of cause and effect relationships. He will find occasions, however, where out of all the possible explanations which might be proposed to account for certain facts, Miss Chute has chosen one with little to commend it aside from its compatibility with her general view of Shakespeare. Although Miss Chute is much less given to axe-grinding than many of Shakespeare's biographers, it is clear that throughout her book she wishes to emphasize what a normal sort of person he was, in spite of his genius. This aim helps to save her from wasting time on some of the far-fetched theories which less cautious biographers have sometimes advanced, but in a few places it involves her in difficulties.

Perhaps her treatment of the peculiar circumstances surrounding Shakespeare's marriage is the most conspicuous example of this tendency in her thinking. At least it is one which can be guaranteed to attract the interest of high school students and provoke some response from them. The documents tell us that when he was just eighteen, Shakespeare married a woman of twenty-six after obtaining a special license which enabled the marriage to take place much more quickly than the normal procedures of that time would otherwise have permitted. An exploration of the couple's need for haste is suggested by the church register at Stratford, which shows that the first child of this marriage was baptized no more than six months after the wedding. Miss Chute recognizes that more than one interpretation of these facts is possible, but she thinks it most probable that Shakespeare and the woman he married "had what was known as a pre-contract and that Anne Hathaway felt free to behave as a married woman before the actual ceremony." The main reason she offers for her choice of this hypothesis is that

> it is not likely that a woman of twenty-six found herself caught in a casual liaison and had to demand marriage to protect herself. Nor is it necessary to believe that she trapped an impressionable young man into marriage by seducing him.

By dismissing these alternative possibilities and proposing the existence of a pre-contract, Miss Chute is able to account for the odd circumstances of this marriage without blaming either William or Anne for anything more than imprudence. The trouble is, though, that neither she nor any of her predecessors has any evidence to support this pre-contract theory; and considered entirely as a hypothesis, it seems no more probable than the "not likely" idea of William's having taken advantage of Anne, and no more "necessary" than the supposition of Anne's having seduced William.

Does any one of these possible explanations really have more to command it than its rivals? It would be interesting to turn a class of high school students loose on this problem to see which theory they would prefer and how many other theories they could invent, employing the talents they like to display as amateur psychologists, marriage counselors, and observers of life. An ideal explanation—if one were possible—might account not only for this marriage, but for the many years of separation which seem to have followed it. Perhaps in the last analysis the whole problem should be dismissed with the Pennsylvania Dutch proverb which the late Professor Edward Hubler of Princeton used to quote whenever he lectured on this topic: "It takes nine months for every baby—except the first." But in any case, we have here a good example of how a biographer's interpretation of certain facts seems to rest mainly on her desire to portray Shakespeare as favorably as possible, and not on a purely objective consideration of these facts themselves. Such opportunities of identifying the biographer's bias, if we may call it that, are by no means in *Shakespeare of London*. If this is the book we choose to show our students how biographies are written and how they should be read, then this opportunity is not one we can afford to waste.

No matter how carefully we scrutinize it for symptoms of un-reliability, however, *Shakespeare of London* remains an admirable book, far superior to most of the biographies which have been written about Shakespeare, including several by scholars who en-joy more renown in academic circles than Marchette Chute. Her book proves, among other things, that popular biographies can be written without sacrificing in any crucial respect the virtue of factual accuracy which is essential to biographies of all kinds. Indeed, many of the features of this book which have the greatest appeal for most readers—such as her vivid description of life in Elizabethan London or her account of what an afternoon at the theatre was like at that time—depend for their fascinating detail not on Miss Chute's imagination but on the facts she has gleaned from dozens of documentary sources. Although her respect for these facts prevents her from exercising the freedom of a novelist to invent striking circumstances or events, it makes it possible for her to write a book which is at once more interesting and more convincing than most novels.

Shakespeare of London also shows how a biographer's fidelity to fact can more than compensate for her inability to match the novelist in other important respects. If this book were a novel, we could properly deplore its failure to realize the personality of its hero more fully than it does. In Miss Chute's pages, the man Shakespeare never seems to stand before us as a living person. His chief actions are recorded there, but his thoughts, motives, fears, and feelings remain obscure. From a novelist we should have every right to expect a more complete characterization.

What would be a token of weakness in fiction, however, can be a sign of strength in biography. The limits of Miss Chute's portrayal of Shakespeare are determined by the nature of her documentary evidence, which records the progress of Shakespeare's career, but not the course of his inner life. To the intelligent reader, therefore, the limits of her characterization enhance, rather than detract from, the value of her book. They testify to her dedication to accuracy, to her distrust of speculation. They confirm our faith in her reliability as a recorder of actual human experience. They earn the reward reserved for that devotion to the *plain truth*, which is the strength and substance of biography.